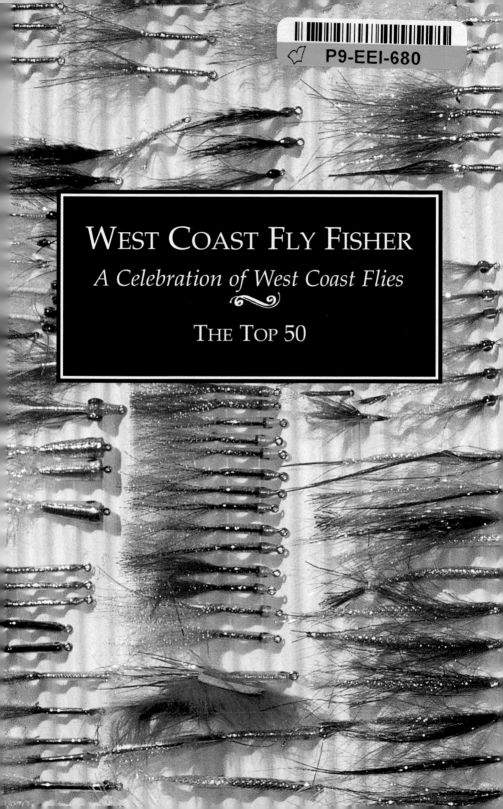

WEST COAST FLY FISHER

A Celebration of West Coast Flies

THE TOP 50

BLOODWORM
Hook: size #14 – #10, 2X
Thread: black or maroon 6/0
Tail: 2 short strands of red super floss
Body: red acetate floss
Rib: holographic silver tinsel
Note: dip completed fly in acetone to set acetate floss

BLACK CHIRONOMID
Hook: curved shrimp hook #16 – #10
Thread: black 8/0
Tail: tuft of white antron fibers
Body: black frostbite or flashabou
Rib: silver tinsel
Thorax: peacock herl
Shellback: pheasant tail
Gills: white antron fibers

GOLD BEAD-HEAD CHIRONOMID
Hook: curved shrimp hook size #16 – #10
Thread: black 8/0
Body: maroon frostbite
Rib: fine silver wire
Collar: peacock herl
Bead: extrasmall gold metal bead
Gills: white antron fibres

Photos (Flies pp. 2-15): Harry Penner

SKIP NYMPH
(*Callibaetis* Mayfly Nymph)
Hook: curved shrimp hook
size #14 – #10, 2X
Thread: black 6/0
Tail: pheasant tail feathers
Body: rabbit antron dubbing
Shellback: pheasant tail fibers
Ribbing: fine copper wire

PARACHUTE CALLIBAETIS MAYFLY DUN
Hook: #14 – #12 fine wire std
Thread: black 8/0
Tail: bear hair fibers
Body: gray sparkle yarn
Wing/Post: deer hair
Hackle: grizzly

LADY MCCONNELL
Hook: size #16 – #10 std
Thread: black 8/0
Tail: white Z-lon fibers with grizzly
hackle tip on top
Underbody: dark gray sparkle yarn
Shellback: deer hair
Hackle: 2 grizzly hackle feathers to
match hook size

GREEN GAMMARUS SHRIMP
Hook: curved shrimp hook
size #14 – #8
Thread: black 6/0
Tail: green synthetic peacock dubbing
Body: green synthetic peacock dubbing
Shellback: olive green stretch-flex
Ribbing: fine silver wire

DRAGONFLY NYMPH
Hook: #10 – #6, 3X long shank
Thread: black 6/0
Body: dark olive synthetic seal fur
Rib: fine gold wire
Shellback: pheasant tail fibers
Legs: ring-necked pheasant rump fibers
Head: peacock herl

TRAVELING SEDGE PUPA
Hook: #10 – #6, 2X long shank
Thread: black 6/0
Body: synthetic seal fur
Rib: bright green super floss
Shellback: pheasant tail fibers
Legs: ring-necked pheasant rump fibers
Head: peacock herl

GREEN DAMSELFLY NYMPH
Hook: #10 – #8 swimming nymph hook
Thread: green 6/0
Tail: marabou fibers
Body: dubbed olive green synthetic seal fur
Rib: fine gold wire
Legs: Hungarian partridge
Shellback: olive green synthetic raffia
Eyes: black plastic

MIKALUK SEDGE
Hook: #10 – #6, 2X fine wire
Thread: black 6/0
Body: synthetic seal fur in olive to dark green
Wings: stacked elk hair
Hackle: ginger

Start keeping a fishing diary not only to record fishing success, but also to detail hatches, water temperature, specific fishing techniques and successful fly patterns. —BRIAN CHAN

WATER BOATMAN
Hook: #14 – #10 std
Thread: black 6/0
Body: yellow sparkle yarn
Legs: black super floss
Shellback: turkey tail lacquered with Dave's Flex-cement

MAROON BEAD HEAD LEECH
Hook: #10 – #6, 2X long shank
Thread: black 6/0
Body: maroon semi-seal or dazzle dubbing
Head: medium-sized gold thread

PLASTIC PEACOCK CHENILLE LEECH
Hook: #10 – #6, 2X long shank
Thread: black 6/0
Tail: black marabou with 4 strands of pearlescent flashabou
Body: plastic peacock chenille
Head: medium copper bead

GENERAL PRACTITIONER (ORANGE)
Hook: #2 – 5/0 low-water salmon
Tail: orange polar bear hair, red-gold pheasant breast feather
Body: orange wool or seal fur
Eyes: golden pheasant tippet feather
Rib: medium, oval, gold tinsel
Hackle: orange cock neck feather
Wing: golden pheasant breast feathers with an overwing of orange-red hen neck feather
Head: black cellire varnish

GENERAL PRACTITIONER (BLACK)
Hook: #2 – 5/0 low-water salmon
Tail: black squirrel tail, red-gold pheasant breast feather
Body: wrap hook shank with lead then black mohair or wool
Eyes: golden pheasant tippet feather
Rib: medium, oval, silver tinsel
Hackle: black cock neck feather
Wing: black spade hackles, larger black wood duck or black hen neck feathers
Head: black cellire varnish

SQUAMISH POACHER
Hook: #2
Tail: sparse orange bucktail
Eyes: green glass
Body: fluorescent orange chenille
Rib: silver or copper wire or fluorescent red-orange thread
Hackle: orange
Wing: fluorescent orange surveyor's tape carapace

STEELHEAD BEE
Hook: #2 – #10
Tail: fox squirrel, quite bushy
Body: equal sections of dark brown, yellow brown wool, silk or seal fur
Hackle: natural brown, ginger or honey, sparse
Wing: fox squirrel, quite bushy, set slightly forward and well divided

BOMBER

Hook: #2 – #6 Wilson dry-fly salmon
Tail: deer hair—natural or other colors
Body: deer hair clipped cigar shaped
Rib: none
Hackle: fly tyer's fancy
Optional Wing: deer hair protruding over eye of hook

DOC SPRATLEY

Hook: #1 – #4 low-water salmon
Tip: fine, oval silver tinsel
Tag: fluorescent green floss
Tail: a few sprigs of guinea fowl
Butt: black ostrich herl
Body: black floss and seal fur with black hackle over front half
Rib: silver oval tinsel
Throat: Guinea fowl
Wing: slender strips of center tail feather from the ring-necked pheasant
Head: Peacock herl

TAYLOR'S GOLDEN SPEY

Hook: #4 – #5/0 low-water salmon
Body: rear one half of hot orange floss and front half of hot orange seal fur
Rib: flat silver tinsel followed by medium, oval tinsel
Hackle: gray heron feather
Throat: golden pheasant red-orange breast feather or lemon wood duck flank feather
Wing: two golden pheasant red-orange breast feather

BLACK SPEY

Hook: #2 – #6 Wilson dry-fly salmon
Tip: fine oval, gold tinsel
Butt: black floss
Tail: red-orange Indian crow-type feather
Body: black floss
Rib: medium or fine gold twist to match hook size
Hackle: black heron or lawful substitute
Throat: teal flank feather
Wing: bronze mallard
Head: black cellire varnish

WOOLLY WORM
Hook: #2/0 – #10 regular salmon
Tail: short tuft of red or orange wool
Body: black chenille
Hackle: grizzly

COWICHAN SPECIAL
Hook: #10 – #4
Tail: a few sprigs from a white hackle
Body: red or orange chenille
Collar: soft, white hackle

COMBO BUG
Hook: #4 or #6 Tiemco TMC 200
Tail: deer hair or none
Body: black foam
Rib: black rod-binding thread
Wing & Throat: deer hair
Collar: deer hair ends

AS SPECIFIED NO. 1 & 2
Hook: #2 – #10 low-water salmon
Tip: fine, gold, oval tinsel
Tag: purple floss
Tail: purple hackle feather
Body: purple floss with purple seal fur
Rib: medium, gold, oval tinsel
Hackel: black hackle feather with one side stripped to maintain sparseness
Throat: teal or widgeon flank feather with one side stripped
Wing: bronze mallard (No. 1), black squirrel (No. 2)
Head: black cellire varnish

Barry Thornton's
Saltwater Salmon Flies

WEIGH WESTER
Created by Bob Jones
Hook: mustad #34011SS or #34007SS, size #1
Thread: white
Body: Mylar piping
Eyes: red
Tail: white polar bear hair
Epoxy: 5 minutes

SILVER THORN DRESSED
Created by Barry M. Thornton
Hook: mustad #34011SS or #34007SS, sizes #1/0, #1, #2, #4, #6
Thread: silver
Body: silver tinsel chenille
Throat: bright red wool, Fishair
Wing: peacock sword
Tail: peacock sword, silver Krystal Flash

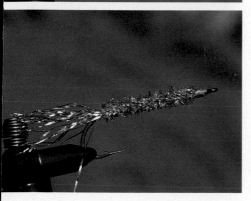

SILVER THORN FLASHTAIL
Hook: mustad #34011SS or #34007SS, sizes #1/0, #1, #2, #4, #6
Thread: silver
Body: silver tinsel chenille
Tail: silver Mylar frayed

PINK EVE
Created by Barry M. Thornton
Hook: mustad #34011SS,
sizes #6, #4 or #2
Thread: MUST be pink
Body: oval tinsel
Head: MUST be pink
(use tying thread to build this)
Variations:
• add pink tail and/or pink wing
• tie as an optic with silver beads or
  pink/red glass beads to add weight

OPTIC SHRIMP
Hook: mustad #34011SS or #34007,
sizes #2, #4, #6
Thread: silver
Body: florescent pink plastic chenille
trimmed on top
Wing: pink fishhair, pink bucktail or
pink polar bear hair
Eyes: silver bead chain

SMILEY NEEDLEFISH (PINK)
Hook: mustad #34007SS, sizes #6 – #2
Body: Mylar piping
Eyes: black
Tail: pink and white polar bear hair
and pink Krystal Flash
Epoxy: 5 minutes

OLE'S HAKAI THORN
Created by Barry M. Thornton
Hook: mustad #34011SS or #340007SS,
sizes #1/0, #1, #2, #4, #6
Thread: silver
Body: silver tinsel chenille
Wing: pink bucktail or pink polar
bear hair
Tail: pearlescent metallic braid

RED HANDLEBAR
Hook: mustad #34011SS or #34007SS, sizes #6 – #2
Thread: pink
Body: pink edge bright
Throat: pink Krystal Flash
Tail: pink Krystal Flash and pink polar bear hair

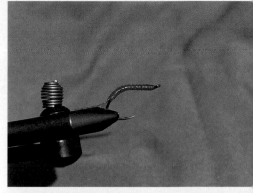

STREAKER
Dressings by Shawn Bennett & Lise Peters
Hook: Mustad #34007 or #34011, sizes #2/0 – #2
Thread: Uni-Mono .004
Body: Mylar tubing, silver or gold
Throat: short red over longer white hair*
Wing: long white hair–*hair can be either polar bear or bucktail
   Peacock sword - Matching Pair
   Krystal Flash - Pink
   Polar Flash - Chartreuse
Eyes: Mylar stick-on 2mm
Head: epoxy

CHARTREUSE CLOUSER
Dressings by Bob Weir
Hook: mustad #34011SS, sizes #1/0 – #4
Thread: white
Wing: polar bear hair, white and yellow, tied over lead eyes and tied off at hook eye; chartreuse polar bear hair and chartreuse crystal flash tied under hook and finish as head
Body: no body
Eyes: lead eyes on top of hook; red or yellow painted eyes
Head: epoxy finish
Tip: tie sparse to medium

PINK BUCKTAIL *Dressings by Bob Weir*
Hook: Tandem set up: mustad #34007; keel #1/0; trailer #4; cut off keel hook at upper bend after tying fly
Thread: white
Wing: sparse, first layer white polar bear, second layer pink deer hair, third layer white polar bear, fourth layer pale mauve, fifth layer pearl crystal flash tied on side of wings; all items tied full length to trailer hook
Head: form and shape red eye with black pupil and epoxy
Body: No body; or Mylar tinsel

Harry Penner's
West Coast River Flies

EPOXY MINNOW
Hook: tiemco 5263 #6
Tail: mallard flank
Body: Mylar with stick on eye
Back: mallard flank, coat entire body
with epoxy

POPSICLE LEECH
Hook: tiemco 7999 #2, #4
Body: pink, orange and purple
marabou tied from middle of hook
shank to head (this fly can also be
tied in chartreuse and kelly green for
sockeye)

ROLLED MUDDLER (NATURAL)
Hook: tiemco 5263 #4, #6, #8
Tail: mallard flank
Body: tinsel
Wing: mallard flank and few strands
crystal flash
Head: spun deer hair

I have always fished with very few patterns, and learned to fish them to the best of my ability. I find if there are too many flies in the fly box, I get a headache from all the self-doubt.
　　　　　　　　　　　　　　　　　　—HARRY PENNER

PINK FLY
Hook: tiemco 93394 #4, #6
Tail: pink marabou
Body: crystal flash with a coating of epoxy

YELLOW PROFESSOR
Hook: tiemco 5263 #6
Tail: tip of saddle hackle (red)
Body: yellow plastic chenille
Wing: teal flank with six strands of crystal flash
Throat: saddle hackle (red or green)

GREEN PROFESSOR
Hook: tiemco 5263 #6
Tail: tip of saddle hackle (red)
Body: green plastic chenille
Wing: teal flank with six strands of crystal flash
Throat: saddle hackle (red or green)

FRASER RIVER STONEFLY
Hook: size #10 – #16, 2X long
Tail: black hackle fibers
Body: black 4 strand floss
Rib: red copper wire
Thorax: peacock herl
Wing Case: pearl accent flashabou
Throat: black hackle fibers (sparse)

EGG-SUCKING LEECH
Hook: size #8 – #12, 3X long
Tail: black marabou
Body: black chenille palmered with
black hackle
Rib: medium copper wire
Front Quarter: fluorescent orange or
fluorescent pink chenille

CUTTHROAT EPOXY MINNOW
Hook: size #6 – #12, 3X long stainless
or nickel plate
Tail: fibers of dyed olive mallard
flank
Body: dyed olive mallard flank tied
down over silver or pearl Mylar tinsel
Eyes: stick-on or painted
Body: body only covered with
Devcon epoxy

GLO-BUG
Hook: size #6 – #8 short shank heavy wire
Thread: kevlar
Body: fluorescent pink, orange, chartreuse, glo-bug yarn

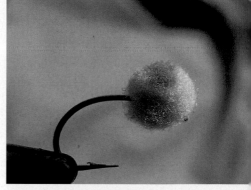

ROLLED MUDDLER
Hook: size #6 – #14, 3X long
Thread: red 6/0
Tail: teal flank
Body: silver or gold #14 flat Mylar tinsel
Wing: deer hair (sparse)
Throat: red 6/0 thread
Head: spun deer hair trimmed down small

TIED DOWN MINNOW
Hook: size 6 – #10, 3X long
Body: silver or pearl small braided Mylar tubing
Thread: olive monocord
Back: dyed olive mallard flank tied down
Throat: red hackle fibers

CUTTHROAT TROUT DRY FLY
Hook: size #8 – #10, 2X long
Tail: deer hair
Body: dubbed amber scintilla dubbing palmered with brown hackle
Wing: tied down deer hair shell back

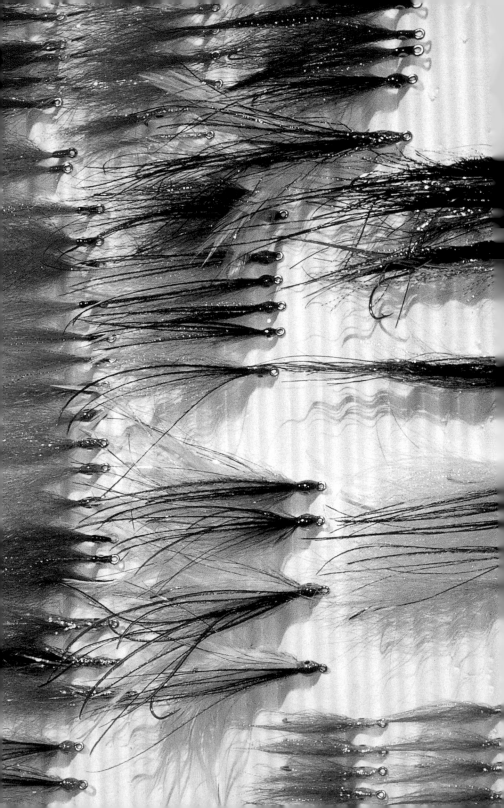

West Coast
Fly Fisher

MAPLE FALLS, WA
Aug. 2002

West Coast Fly Fisher

Brian Chan
Kelly Davison
Art Lingren
Harry Penner
Barry M. Thornton

Compiled by Mark Pendlington

hancock
house

ISBN 0-88839-440-3 softcover
ISBN 0-88839-448-9 hardcover limited edition
Copyright © Ocean West Group Ltd.

Cataloging in Publication Data
West Coast fly fisher

ISBN 0-88839-440-3 softcover
ISBN 0-88839-448-9 hardcover limited edition

1. Fly fishing—British Columbia. 2. Fly Fishing—British
Columbia—Pictorial works. I. Thornton, Barry M. II.
Pendlington, Mark.
SH572.B8W47 1998   799.1'24'09711   C98-910636-5

Editor: Nancy Miller
Production: Ingrid Luters
Cover Photo: Harry Penner

Published simultaneously in Canada and the United States by

HANCOCK HOUSE PUBLISHERS LTD.
19313 Zero Avenue, Surrey, B.C. V4P 1M7
(604) 538-1114 Fax (604) 538-2262

HANCOCK HOUSE PUBLISHERS
1431 Harrison Avenue, Blaine, WA 98230
(604) 538-1114 Fax (604) 538-2262
Web Site: www.hancockhouse.com *email:* sales@hancockhouse.com

Contents

Index

Acknowledgments

I would like to thank all of the authors and photographers who have given their time to make this book possible. I am also indebted to them for sharing their experiences in teaching us how to fly fish the West Coast the right way.

Dedication

This book is dedicated to my parents, Alan and Shirley Pendlington, for giving me the chance to always be near rivers; my wife Jacqueline for putting up with me and letting me pursue my passion year after year; also, my brothers Stephen and Andrew Pendlington. And to Brad and Jennifer Pendlington, may you experience the joys of life that you have brought to me. Finally, this book is dedicated to all fly fishers that truly understand the word conservation and believe that letting their fish go really does make a difference to the future of the wonderful sport of fly fishing.

The Authors

Brian Chan

Professional author and fisheries biologist, Brian Chan enjoys a work career that focuses on a subject that is also his passion For the past twenty-four years, Brian has worked on trout management in B.C.'s Kamloops region, focusing on the thousands of productive lakes that dot the province's southern interior. Brian has been an ardent fly fisher for the past thirty years and has been active in conservation efforts. He has authored *Flyfishing Strategies for Stillwaters* and contributed to *The Gilly*. His fly-tying abilities were also featured in *The World's Best Trout Flies* and he has also produced two volumes of an instructional video series on lake fly fishing.

Arthur Lingren

Through most of his adult life, Art Lingren has been involved in the fishing community. He is a member and past president of the Totem Flyfishers, an honorary member of the Loons Fly Fishing Club, a long-time member of the B.C. Federation of Fly Fisher (BCFFF) acting as their historian and vice-chair, and has served many years as a director of the Steelhead Society of B.C. He has been awarded the BCFFF's Angul Award, given to B.C. fly fishers who show an appreciation for the ancestry of fly fishing and its development. Art's books include *Fly Patterns of Roderick Haig-Brown*, *River Journal: Thompson River*, *Fly Patterns of British Columbia*, *Irresistible Waters: Fly Fishing in B.C. Throughout the Year,* and *River Journal: Dean River.*

Barry Thornton

Barry Thornton is one of B.C.'s best known outdoor writers. Involved with fishing and the outdoors as a professional educator, writer and photographer, he is the author of *Steelhead, Saltwater Fly Fishing for Pacific Salmon* and *Salgair: A Steelhead Odyssey* (all Hancock House publications). Barry currently writes fishing and outdoor articles for regional, national and international magazines and newspapers and on the internet. His articles have received awards from the Outdoor Writers of Canada and the Northwest Outdoor Writer's Association. His writing has also been recognized by the American Fisheries Society Northwest Chapter with the Roderick Haig-Brown Memorial Award. He is a founding chairman and three-time elected president of the Steelhead Society of B.C.

Kelly Davison

Kelly Davison has been guiding and teaching fly fishing on the south coast of B.C. most of his adult life. He is an active member of the Steelhead Society of B.C. and the B.C. Federation of Fly Fishers. Kelly is well known for his active television career, completing five primetime programs for the *Sportfishing British Columbia* series.

Harry Penner

A talented south coast guide, Harry Penner has been fly casting coastal rivers for years. In addition to guiding, Harry writes articles and supplies spectacular nature photographs for various outdoor publications. He also enjoys sharing his no-nonsense fishing approach with viewers of the *Sportfishing British Columbia* television series.

Preface

I have had the extreme privilege and pleasure of fishing with some of the most knowledgeable fly fishers in British Columbia, and in turn sharing these experiences with millions of Canadians each year. The pages of this book hold more than 100 collective years of fly fishing experience, delivered by some of the finest fly fishers within their specific discipline. The *West Coast Fly Fisher* was designed to provide fly fishers with an invaluable source of useful information that could become a reference companion at water's edge; to motivate and enable readers to learn from the masters; and to allow readers to to take their fly fishing to new levels.

Brian Chan has become one of the most knowledgeable still water anglers of our time. He shares his unique understanding of a lake environment and takes a comprehensive look at lake entomology, productive zones, hatches and trip timing—critical concerns if one ever hopes to master fly fishing the lakes of the Pacific Northwest.

Arthur Lingren has an intimate understanding of how to read a river and where steelhead like to hold in a river's riffles and runs. Fly fishing for the majestic steelhead is as difficult an angling challenge as it gets, and Art's written description of techniques, history, strategies, fly patterns, migration and timing, reading water and the beautiful steelhead flies he calls his Magic Dozen are second to none.

When it comes to one of the most exciting and adrenaline-pumping aspects of fly fishing the West, it would have to be saltwater fly fishing the Pacific Ocean for silver bright cruising coho and chinook salmon. In his chapter, Barry Thornton shares his extensive knowledge of coho and chinook salmon in open saltwater and the beaches and estuaries of the Pacific Rim. He covers estuary and feeder salmon strategies, hunting coho and chinook, open-water anchoring and the most productive saltwater flies.

Professional guide Kelly Davison shares his passion by taking readers through the "seasons of the sea-run cutthroat trout" in its freshwater and saltwater environments explaining the different habitats of the sea-run cutthroat, food sources, trip timing, equipment as well as the productive fly patterns to use.

Harry Penner details his professional guiding techniques for fly casting to salmon on the West Coast rivers. His methods take a no-nonsense approach, utilizing specific flies, lines, gear and casting techniques and he offers an in-depth look at reading fly water for all five of the Pacific salmon species.

I am thrilled to have the opportunity to offer readers one of the most comprehensive fly fishing books ever written, with eye-bursting pictures that truly are a celebration of the West Coast, its premier sport fish and its finest fly fishers. Enjoy!

MARK PENDLINGTON, 1998

Fly Fishing the Pacific Northwest Lakes

by Brian Chan

The Resource

The West Coast is blessed with an incredible abundance of freshwater fishing opportunities. One of the richest fishing resources we have is the tremendous number of lakes scattered throughout the Pacific Northwest. Some of the best trout fishing in North America, and for that matter the world, is found in the interior regions of the Northwest, particularly that vast expanse of land that lies between the coast mountains on the west and the Rocky Mountain Range on the east. The most fertile waters are found from the Prince George area south to the border with the states of Washington and Montana. There are literally thousands of small lakes scattered from valley bottoms to mountain peaks containing populations of rainbow trout, brook trout and kokanee salmon. Many of the most productive lakes were created when the glaciers receded thousands of years ago. Nutrient-rich water, relatively shallow depths and long growing seasons provide the right ingredients to grow some very large fish. The result is a Mecca for the fly rod enthusiast.

Access to these waters varies from highway to difficult four-wheel-drive roads to hike- or fly-in situations. The majority of these lakes support wild populations of rainbow trout and considerable management effort is expended to protect and maintain the genetic diversity of these waters. However, many of the more popular and most accessible fishing lakes are landlocked or do not have adequate spawning streams for trout to reproduce naturally. The provincial government operates hatchery facilities that provide rainbow trout and brook trout for regular stocking programs in these highly productive lakes. Stocking rates are carefully manipulated to create various types of fishing opportunities ranging from abundant populations of small fish to smaller numbers of very large fish.

Basic Lake Biology

Becoming a successful lake or stillwater fly fisher is made much easier if one has some basic knowledge of lake biology and the seasonal changes that occur within a lake. This biology lesson will explain why fish inhabit and feed in certain parts of a lake at different times of the year. It will also make it much easier to learn about trout food sources and aquatic insect hatches.

Lake structure

The typical small lake is saucer shaped, having deeper water in the middle and shallow areas around the edges. The shallow water area of the lake is known as the shoal or littoral zone (see fig. I).

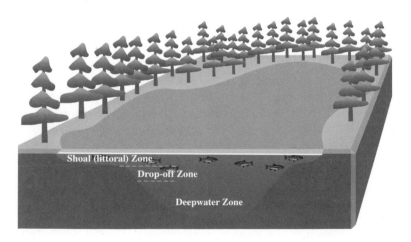

FIGURE I: Cross-sectional view of a typical small lake.

The water gradually deepens as one moves into the middle or deepwater zone of the lake and then begins to shallow again as the other shoreline approaches. The shoal is defined as that depth zone of a lake where sunlight can penetrate to the bottom and allow photosynthesis to grow rooted plants such as cattails, bulrush, lily pads, pond weed and milfoil. This lush plant life provides excellent habitat for aquatic insects, crustaceans and other trout food. Shoal habitats typically extend out to water that reaches a maximum of eighteen to twenty-five feet in depth. Trout spend the majority of their feeding time on the shoal! As the water deepens it passes through a transition zone called the drop-off (see fig. I). The drop-off signals the end of the shoal and beginning of the deepwater zone. Drop-offs are especially important to trout as refuge areas to avoid predators and to escape warm shoal water temperatures during midsummer conditions. The deepwater zone often makes up the largest volume of the lake; it is an important trout habitat in the late spring and fall when oxygen levels are adequate.

Seasons of a lake
Small lakes undergo the seasonal changes of spring, summer, fall and winter. Oxygen and temperature levels that vary with the season are affected by the mixing action of the water that also occurs at specific times of the year. All these factors have a significant bearing on where trout live and feed. Anglers that understand these seasonal changes will know exactly what depth zones trout can live in at various times of the year and therefore concentrate their fishing efforts accordingly.

Winter: Let's first look at a typical interior lake during the winter season (see fig. II). A thick covering of ice and snow prevents any photosynthesis from occurring, so plant life that grew on the shoals during the open-water period dies back and decomposes. Oxygen is used during the decomposition process and as winter progresses there are decreasing amounts available to support fish and other organisms. Near the end of winter there is often only a narrow band of oxygenated water located immediately below the ice. This results in fish being confined to a shallow zone of water until well after ice off.

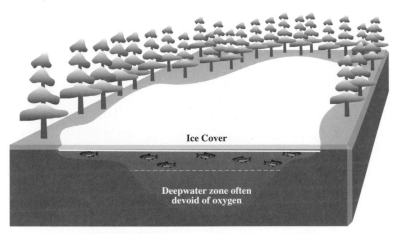

FIGURE II: Mid-winter conditions in a small lake.

Spring: At ice off, a lake does not immediately mix because of some unique thermal characteristics of water. Surface waters are cooler than those close to the lake bottom and the differences in temperature resist mixing. This means that in many lakes, for a certain length of time after ice off, trout are still confined to that band of oxygenated water immediately below the surface of the lake. Knowledgeable anglers watch local lakes closely so they can be on the lake as the ice is leaving. It generally takes one to two weeks for the early spring sun to warm the upper layers of water to the same temperature as the deeper water. Once the water temperature is uniform from top to bottom, a good strong wind will create circulating currents that move surface waters to the bottom and vice versa (see fig. III).

Water sinks or moves easily when it reaches 39°F. This mixing is called turnover, and in small lakes it occurs in the early spring and again late in the fall. When a lake turns over, bottom debris and vegetation is swept up and mixed throughout the water column. This results in very turbid or off-colored water. Trout and other fish species are affected by turnover as overall oxygen levels drop and other gases are mixed into the water column. It can take up to two weeks for the water to clear and fish to actively resume feeding. The completion of

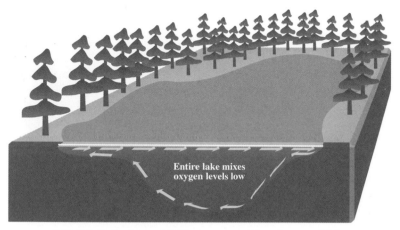

Entire lake mixes oxygen levels low

FIGURE III: Spring and fall turnover conditions in a small lake.

spring turnover signals the start of the major insect hatches and some of the best fishing opportunities of the year.

Summer: The lake water continues to warm up through the spring and into the summer period. Aquatic vegetation growth flourishes on the shoals, insects continue to hatch and the trout partake in the feast. By midsummer a condition known as stratification develops on many small, productive lakes. It results from the fact that the energy of the sun can only warm water to a certain depth. Beyond this depth the water will remain much colder. The depth at which the warm upper layers of water meet the cold deeper water is called the thermocline (see fig. IV). Dive into a lake in midsummer and you quickly find out at what depth the thermocline is located. The clarity of individual lakes determines how deep the thermocline is positioned. Clear water lakes have deeper thermoclines than those that are turbid or murky. Most thermoclines establish between fifteen and twenty feet in depth. During the hottest part of the summer, trout and other fish species will congregate along the upper edge of the thermocline as the water is cooler and better oxygenated than shallower water on the shoal. Thermoclines form an invisible barrier to mixing. Water above the thermocline will mix freely all summer, but even strong winds cannot break through this barrier to

33

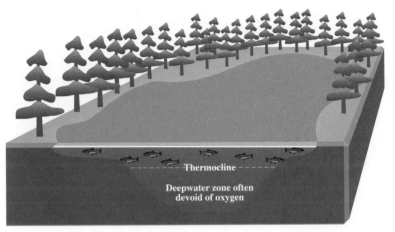

FIGURE IV: Summer stratification conditions in a small lake.

mix the deeper water. Continual decomposition processes occurring on the lake bottom result in significantly reduced oxygen levels in the water below the thermocline. Oxygen levels may become so low that fish life cannot be sustained at those depths. This is an important point for anglers to understand. During the height of summer in many lakes there may not be enough oxygen to support fish below the thermocline.

Fall: Fall air temperatures begin to cool the surface waters of the lake and prepare it for another turnover event. Mixing occurs again when the thermocline breaks down and the lake reaches a uniform temperature from top to bottom. As in the spring, the water will become cloudy or off-colored and changes in water chemistry can put fish off feeding for up to two weeks. The completion of fall turnover triggers the start of some of the most aggressive feeding of the year (see fig. V). Trout sense the pending winter and feed heavily, often in very shallow water, right up until the lake is covered in ice.

Rods, Reels and Fly Lines

Lake fly fishing equipment requirements can be as basic as owning one fly rod, one reel with two spare spools (for other fly lines) and three different fly lines. It is most important that the fly rod and lines are matched or balanced so that a

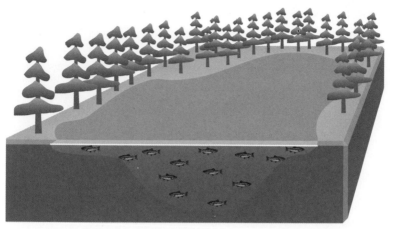

FIGURE V: Late spring and fall conditions in a small lake (post turnover).

proper cast can be completed. Beginners purchasing equipment should seek assistance from businesses that specialize in this sport. A good lake fly rod will be nine to ten feet in length and matched or balanced to #6 or #7 weight fly lines so that a proper casting stroke can be attained. Graphite fly rods have made fly casting and fly fishing a lot more fun because of their lightweight construction and the forgiving nature of the material.

Match your fly rod to three basic fly lines: full floating, slow or intermediate sinking and fast sinking. Floating lines can be used in many of the fishing situations encountered on still waters. Obviously, they are the line to use for imitating adult insects that are sitting on the surface of the lake. However, floating lines are also very effective when fishing with the larval, pupal and nymphal stages of insects that live within the bottom habitat of the shoal zone. Many of the insect hatches will occur in water less than fifteen feet deep and the floating line can be used comfortably with leaders up to eighteen feet in length to cover most areas of the shoal. Weighted flies are often used in combination with long leaders to reduce the time it takes for the fly to reach the deeper depths.

Slow- or intermediate-sinking fly lines sink at a rate of 1.25 to 1.75 inches/second. It is a good line for fishing the mayfly nymph, damselfly nymph and caddisfly pupa flies, since all of these insects begin their emergence journey from the bottom of the shoal to the water's surface.

Fast-sinking fly lines sink at a rate of 3.25 to 4.5 inches/second. This is the line to use when you want to get a dragonfly nymph or leech down deep along the outer edge of the drop-off. It's also the line that imitates the swimming action of water boatmen and back swimmers as they dive down to the bottom of the lake in deep water.

Make sure your reels have at least 200 feet of Dacron backing attached to the end of the fly line just in case you hook the fish of your life. A tapered nylon or braided nylon leader connects the fly line to the fly. Leaders allow the fly to "turnover" and land softly on the water when casting. Leaders can be as short as three feet and more than twenty feet in length, depending on the fly line used, depth of water fished and food source being imitated. Most commercially tied leaders are manufactured in nine-, twelve- and fifteen-meter lengths. The piece of leader that the fly is actually tied on to is called the tippet section. The majority of stillwater angling situations require tippet strengths of between three- and six-pound test. Modern tippet material is manufactured in very fine diameters which allows one to use much stronger material and not affect the action of the fly as it is retrieved through the water.

Trout Food Sources and How to Successfully Fish Them

Trout eat a wide variety of food items, which allows them to grow rapidly and attain large sizes in the most productive waters. Preferred diet items include aquatic and terrestrial insects, crustaceans (shrimp), annelids (leeches), forage fish and zooplankton. Fortunately for the angler, trout don't eat all these creatures at the same time. Some of these food items are available at all times of the year, while others become primary food sources at very specific times such as a particular hatch or migration movement. The task of determining what the trout are feeding on at a particular time of the year is made easier by the fact that the aquatic insects hatch in a sequence based on water temperature and specific insect emergence requirements. For instance, chironomids or midges are always the first insect hatch of the year on British Columbia lakes and on other similar-sized lakes throughout North America. Mayfly hatches typically follow the chironomids and damselflies follow the mayflies and so on. The actual time of year these hatches begin varies as a result of differences in climatic conditions. As a general rule, the first major insect hatches of any kind do not occur until the surface water temperatures reach between 47° and 50°F). Another point to remember is that the majority of lake-dwelling insects hatch or emerge during daylight hours and generally between 10 A.M. and 4 P.M. The major exceptions to this rule are some species of caddis that hatch at night.

Shrimp
Freshwater shrimp are a staple food source in many productive interior lakes. Shrimp are available year round, but are most sought after in early spring prior to the start of the major insect hatches and in late fall when other invertebrates are less abundant. There are two types of shrimp found in interior Northwest lakes. *Gammarus* will reach more than three-quarters of an inch in body length while *Hyalella* is seldom longer than one-eighth of an inch in length. Both shrimp require high levels of calcium in the water to survive. Calcium forms the chitinous exoskeleton of the shrimp body. Shrimp live among the vegetation and debris covering the bottom of the shoal zone. They swim in short two- to six-inch-long pulses and pause regularly for a rest. Their body color varies with that of the habitat in which they live. The most common colors encountered are pale green to dark olive green. Shrimp reproduce numerous times a year and pregnant females are identified by having a bright orange brood pouch located on the underside of the body.

Shrimp imitations can be fished on both floating and sinking fly lines. Slow- or intermediate-sinking lines work well in presenting and keeping shrimp patterns close to the lake bottom. Use a countdown method to determine where your fly is in relation to the bottom of the lake. Use the sink rate of your fly line and calculate the approximate time it will take to reach the bottom of the lake at the depth you are anchored. For instance, an extrafast-sinking line matched to a 6-weight fly rod will sink at approximately four inches per second. Sinking rate information is usually found on the box that a fly line comes in. If you were anchored in twenty-five feet of water, it would take this particular fly line about seventy-five seconds to reach the bottom (25 ft. X 12 inches = 300 inches divided by 4 inches/sec sink rate = 75 sec). If you snag bottom on the first few retrieves, shorten the time you wait on the next casts. Weighted shrimp patterns and long leaders work well with a floating line. Again, allow enough time for the fly to reach the bottom before initiating the retrieve. Your retrieve should consist of slow three- to six-inch-long pulls with frequent pauses, and it's always good to add an occasional series of several short, quick pulls to further attract any nearby fish.

Chironomids

Chironomids are the most abundant family of insects found in lakes. There are more than 1,000 species of these small, two-winged insects identified in North America alone. To the uninitiated, adult chironomids look like adult mosquitoes but the female chironmomid does not bite! Chironomids have a complete life cycle or metamorphosis consisting of the egg, larva, pupa and adult stage. Trout love to feed on the last three life phases. Chironomid species range in size from minute to almost one inch in body length. They come in a wide range of colors with the most common being black, shades of brown, green, orange and maroon.

Chironomids are the most prolonged hatch of the year and can be successfully fished in any month of the open-water period. The most intense hatches occur from early May to the middle of July. The chironomid life cycle begins with egg-laden females returning to the lake. The female flies over the surface of the lake with the tip of her abdomen in the surface film releasing eggs, which sink to the bottom. The eggs hatch into the larval form which live in a tube at the bottom of the lake. Larvae feed on organic material that passes by their tube. The larvae are capable of leaving the tube and searching for food but they are very poor swimmers and become quite vulnerable to predation. Some chironomid larvae have a hemoglobinlike substance in their body that allows them to survive in poorly oxygenated water. These larvae are bright red or maroon in color and trout will often root them out of the bottom of the lake. Other chironomid larvae colors include light green and dark brown. When the larva is fully developed, it will seal off the tube and transform into the pupal stage. The fully developed pupa then breaks out of the tube or cocoon and begins rising to the surface of the lake. Its passage is made easier by gases trapped under its thorax and abdomen. Once the pupa reaches the surface film, a split forms along the back of its thorax and the adult chironomid emerges and flies off to mate. Most chironomid hatches occur on the shoal area in water less than twenty feet deep, but emergences can occur in depths in excess of fifty feet.

A floating fly line in combination with varying leader lengths is an excellent choice of tackle to imitate the chironomid larvae stage and pupal emergences. The floating line acts as a long bobber and the varying leader lengths allow fishing at different depths on the shoal zone. It is a good idea to have some weighted fly patterns to reduce the amount of time required to wait for your fly to sink close to the bottom. The retrieve of both larval and pupal patterns is dead slow or none at all. A strike indicator is often used to suspend a pupal pattern at a precise depth as trout will often feed in a very narrow zone. When chironomids are hatching in the deepwater zone (twenty-five feet) use a full-sinking line and cast it out to the depth in which you are anchored, allow the line to sink until it is vertical in the water column and then begin a dead slow retrieve. This will imitate exactly the pupal rise to the surface of the lake.

Mayflies
The first adult mayflies often begin appearing while the chironomid hatches are still in full swing. The most common genus of mayflies found in interior waters is the *Callibaetis* or speckle-winged variety. Mayflies undergo an incomplete

metamorphosis of egg, nymph and adult stages. The *Callibaetis* nymphs live among the vegetation and bottom cover of the shoal and drop-off zones. Here they graze on algae and other minute organisms. Trout will feed on immature nymphs but prefer to focus on the mature nymphs as they swim to the surface of the lake to emerge into the adult form. Fully mature *Callibaetis* nymphs will reach more than half an inch in length and are easily identified by their very swollen dark wing pads. The newly emerged adult is referred to as the dun or sub-imago stage. This is the nonreproductive phase of the mayfly life cycle. Trout actively search out the duns as they sit on the water drying their wings. Within twenty-four hours of hatching, the dun will undergo a final molt and the reproductive form called the spinner or imago stage emerges. The easiest way to differentiate between duns and spinners is by the color of their wings. Duns have opaque or mottle-colored wings and spinners have clear wings. Mating occurs in large swarming masses that gather along the edge of the lake. Egg-laden females return to the lake to deposit eggs. The females die on the water after egg laying is completed. They are then referred to as spent spinners and are a favorite food of trout.

The emergence swim of the nymphs is best imitated with slow/intermediate-sinking or floating fly lines. After casting, wait for the mayfly nymph to sink close to the bottom of the shoal before beginning a retrieve consisting of three to six-inch long, slow, hand strips (pulling the fly line in by hand). Switch to the adult dun patterns using a floating line when you see trout consistently slashing or boiling at the surface. It's often best to let your dun pattern sit on the water or drift in the wind rather than retrieving it to the boat.

Damselflies
Damselflies and caddisflies are the next insect hatches to appear after the mayflies. Often, they will hatch simultaneously, which is why anglers must constantly look into and around the water for signs of an emergence. Prime damselfly hatches occur from mid-June to mid-July. Damselfly nymphs can easily be identified by their long, slender body and three paddle-shaped tails. They swim in a side-to-side motion and

pause frequently to rest. Their preferred habitat is the shoal zone where there is abundant vegetation to both hide in and seek food. The most common nymphal colors are various shades of green. Individuals will match their color to that of the surrounding habitat. Damselflies can stay in the nymphal stage for up to two years before emerging into the adult phase. Mature or fully developed nymphs swim off the bottom to within three feet of the surface. They then swim toward a bulrush or cattail patch and crawl up out of the water on the stems of the plants. The adult form emerges from the old nymphal shuck. The newly emerged adults soon fly off to shoreline vegetation. Fertilized females fly back to the lake and typically crawl down to the base of emergent plant stems to deposit eggs. Trout feed aggressively on the migrating nymphs and on the newly emerged adults as they cling to plant stems. Often, this means fish will be feeding in water less than three feet deep. At other times gusty winds will knock the adults into the water making easy meals for cruising trout.

The damselfly nymph migration is best imitated with either floating or slow/intermediate-sinking fly lines. Start with the sinking line first as trout will often prefer to feed closer to the bottom than higher in the water column to avoid predators. Switch to the floating line as the hatch intensifies and more of the naturals are closer to the surface of the lake. Try a slow strip or hand twist retrieve of four- to six-inch lengths and give your rod tip an occasional sideways twitch to imitate that sinusoidal movement of the nymph. Always watch for those fish that feed right into the bulrush and cattail patches.

Caddisflies

Caddisfly or sedge hatches are synonymous with big trout slashing and boiling over newly emerged adults as the flies scamper across the water in an attempt to get airborne. Adult caddis fishing is truly the best dry fly fishing opportunity of the year. Watch for this hatch to occur from mid-June to the end of July. Caddisflies exhibit a complete metamorphosis of egg, larva, pupa and adult stage. The caddis larva is easily recognized as the insect that lives in a case built of bits of vegetation or particles of sand and leaves a trail as it crawls along the bottom of the shoal. Larvae feed on vegetation and other organic matter and will travel considerable distances in search of new feeding opportunities. Trout will often seek out the larvae and consume both insect and case. Larvae of the large traveling sedge reach almost one and a half inches in length which gives you an idea of how large the adults will be. Some caddis species will stay in the larval stage for up to two years before transforming into the pupal stage. The larva seals the end of its case and three to six weeks later it will have transformed into the pupal form. The fully developed pupa chews it way out of the old larval case and, with the aid of a pair of oar-shaped legs, swims rapidly to the surface of the lake. Trout actively hunt down the swimming caddis pupae. At the surface, the pupal shuck splits open and the adult form emerges. The newly emerged adults sit on the water momentarily to dry their wings before running a short distance across the water and taking flight.

Caddis larvae patterns are best fished on slow/intermediate-sinking lines. Use a very slow strip retrieve and try to keep the fly as close to the lake bottom as possible. The swimming caddis pupa is also imitated well by the intermediate-sinking line. In this case, allow the fly to sink close to the bottom of the shoal and then retrieve right to the surface in six- to eight-inch-long quick strips. A floating line and long leader can also be effective in imitating the pupal swim; again use a quick-strip retrieve. As the trout start feeding on the adults switch to a floating line and the dry caddis imitation. Try a retrieve of continuous, quick, two- to six-inch-long strips and keep a sharp eye on the fly.

Dragonflies
Dragonflies are the last major insect emergence of the season. They typically begin hatching in early July and will emerge right through to the end of September. These close cousins of the damselfly can live for up to four years as a nymph before transforming into the familiar adult stage. Two families of dragonflies are regularly found in interior lakes. The *Aeshnid* or Darner dragonfly nymph has a relatively slender body that can reach almost two inches in length. It is an active swimmer

and hunts down shrimp, mayfly and damselfly nymphs that are hiding in the vegetation covering the shoal area of the lake. The *Libelludid* or sprawler dragonfly nymph is much shorter and wider in body shape. Sprawler nymphs camouflage themselves in the silt and bottom debris and ambush their prey. Dragonfly nymphs have a retractable lower lip that they extend out to capture prey. These nymphs are capable of quick forward movement by taking in water and expelling it through the tip of their abdomen. Trout are able to feed on immature dragonfly nymphs at any time of the year, providing they can catch them among the thick bottom vegetation. Fish really key in on mature nymphs as they crawl or swim along the bottom of the shoal toward shore to emerge as adults. At shore the nymphs crawl out of the water and climb up the stalks or stems of plants. The nymphal skin splits open and the adult winged dragonfly crawls out. Adult dragonflies will live for several months feeding on other smaller flying insects including mosquitoes.

Fast-sinking fly lines work well in imitating these large food items as they crawl or swim along the bottom of the shoal and drop-off. Use the countdown method to ensure that your fly is in the bottom zone as you retrieve, so it is exposed to as many fish as possible. Try a moderately slow retrieve of three- to six-inch-long strips. Remember to try dragonfly nymphs when searching out a new lake as these insects are available to trout at all times of the year.

Water Boatmen and Backswimmers

Water boatmen and backswimmers are air-breathing insects that trout feed on during the spring and late fall months. Both insects have an elongated, oar-shaped pair of legs that allows them to swim rapidly through the water. Water boatmen, also called water bugs, are the smaller of the two insects, seldom reaching more than a quarter inch in length, while back swimmers can measure as long as half an inch. Preferred habitat is the shallow areas of the shoal zone where they feed on smaller insects and shrimp. They trap air against their abdomen, which appears as a shiny or silvery bubble. Adults form mating and swarming flights in the spring and fall. Large numbers of boatmen and back swimmers will fly from one lake and dive into another creating a "rain" effect. Trout will slash at the insects as they hit the water and then chase them while the insects swim down to lay eggs and return to the surface again to breathe.

The classic technique to imitate these diving insects is to cast a fast- or extrafast-sinking fly line as far as possible with a boatman or backswimmer pattern. When a regular sinking fly line descends, it forms a belly or bow as the heavier or thicker portions of the line sink faster than the tip section. This creates an open U-shaped line in the water. Stripping the line in pulls the pattern down and then back up just like the actual swimming insects. Use a retrieve consisting of continuous two- to four-inch-long fast hand strips. In the early spring period, try fishing these insects with floating or slow-sinking lines in the very shallow portions of the shoal.

Terrestrial Insects

Carpenter ants, termites, grasshoppers and bees often become unwilling trout food when they get blown onto or fall into a lake. Ants and termites regularly form mating and swarming flights and inevitably land on interior lakes. Mountain pine beetles and spruce bark beetles also make swarming flights that take them over water. Carry at least a few ant patterns and small, dark brown beetle imitations in your fly box as you never know when a hatch will appear. You should also expect to see grasshopper activity when fishing low elevation grassland lakes on hot summer days. Trout feeding on terrestrials in the surface film will show slashing or boiling rise forms. Use a floating line with the appropriate-sized imitation and either cast ahead of a working fish and retrieve the fly as it lands on the water or let it drift with the wind and wait for a fish to intercept it.

Leeches

Leeches are another food source that are available for trout to feed on at all times of the year. These flattened, segmented worms are found in almost all small lake environments. They can reach more than six inches in length when fully extended and swimming. Leeches are scavengers and are most commonly found hiding under rocks or logs at the bottom of the shoal zone. Their body coloration includes black, brown, green, maroon and mottled variations of these colors. They are preferred trout food during the spring months, at night during the hot summer period, and late in the fall when other food items are less abundant.

Leech patterns can be fished on floating or any type of sinking line. During the daytime, try fishing leeches parallel or perpendicular to the edge of the drop-off with slow- and fast-sinking lines and a very slow strip retrieve. In the evening or at night, move into the shallow parts of the shoal and try leeches on a floating line. Use a nine-foot-long leader with at least a six-pound tippet strength, as these shallow water trout hit hard when feeding under the cover of darkness.

Forage Fish

Many interior Northwest lakes support populations of both trout and other nongame fish species such as suckers, shiners, sculpins and chub. These fish can be an important food source for the native populations of trout. Forage fish often travel in large schools and cruise through the lush vegetation of the shoal in search of food. They make ideal targets for single or small groups of piscivorous (fish-eating) trout. The telltale sign of a trout chasing down forage fish is the spray of baitfish as they frantically attempt to evade certain death. Look for this feeding pattern during the hot summer period and particularly in the early evening hours. Take a close look at the size and coloration of the forage fish and match your pattern as closely as possible. Forage fish imitations can be fished on both floating and sinking fly lines. The key to success is locating and staying as close as possible to the schools of bait fish without scaring them off. This technique is best accomplished with two people in a boat, as both can take turns fishing or handling the oars or motor. Using a fast- or extrafast-sinking line, cast to the outside edge of the school, wait for the fly to sink below the fish and then initiate a very quick strip retrieve back up to the surface. The floating line technique usually works by casting ahead of a working trout and quickly stripping the fly past the feeding fish.

Fishing Craft

The majority of small lake fishing opportunities encountered will require a boat or other floating craft so that you can access the shoals or drop-off zones of a lake. Flat-bottomed prams are ideal for fishing small lakes as they are lightweight, maneuverable and offer a very stable casting platform. Fishing from a boat gives you a higher vantage point to look into the water for cruising fish or insect hatches. Float tubes and pontoon boats are also very popular on small lakes. These one-person inflatable fishing crafts are very light, compact when deflated and can be backpacked into lakes that are inaccessible by roads. They are a relatively inexpensive way to get on the water. Their main disadvantage is the low profile on the water which prevents the angler from seeing any distance into the water. Regardless of the type of craft you are fishing from, remember to have a pair of Polaroid sunglasses handy so that you can see through the glare on the water. You will also need to equip your boat with anchors for the bow and stern so that it will not move with changes in wind direction. This allows you to maintain full control while retrieving your fly line and fly so that strikes can be better detected. A two-pound lead downrigger ball or trolling weight works well for a float tube anchor. It is also a good idea to mark off your anchor rope every meter with a waterproof pen so that you know the depth of water you are fishing.

Searching Out a New Lake

Even very small lakes can be intimidating when it is your first time on that body of water. A good way to learn about a new lake is to troll a fly around the edges of the drop-off and shoal zones. Use fast- and extrafast-sinking fly lines to get your fly down to the bottom of these two zones. Dragonfly nymphs and leeches are excellent searching patterns. (Searching fly patterns means using flies that represent common trout food sources, with which the fish are familiar, found in almost all small lakes.) If you are fishing

46

from a boat, use the oars to control your speed and direction. Take a few slow strokes of the oars and then let the boat drift for five to ten seconds. This lets the fly sink back down close to the bottom. Resume a slow row and the fly slowly rises up in the water column. Make sure your rod is securely placed in the boat so that a hard strike does not take it overboard. Float tubes and pontoon boats are ideal for trolling flies as you can have even greater control of your speed via the effort in kicking your fins.

If the lake has clear water you will quickly get a feel for its shape and structure. Mentally record where the big shoal areas and sunken islands are as they will be the places to fish more seriously later in the day. Keep an eye in the water and on the surface of the lake for insect hatches or other food sources. A depth sounder, or fish finder, can be an invaluable tool in determining the underwater structure of a body of water, especially if it is dark or tannic stained and the bottom of the shoal and edges of the drop-off cannot be seen. Remember, during the midsummer period the deep portions of the lake may not be frequented by fish.

Wrapping It Up

The abundance of small lakes in the Pacific Northwest offers anglers a lifetime of fishing opportunities. Every day spent on the water is an ongoing learning experience. Knowing the seasonal changes that lakes undergo and understanding the life cycles and habitat requirements of what trout eat provide a good foundation for mastering this unique style of fly fishing.

The importance of being observant, whether at the water's edge or out on the water, cannot be overemphasized. So much of what Mother Nature does is visible to the human eye. The challenge in stillwater fly fishing is determining what the trout are going to eat on that particular day. The little clues that an angler observes help to solve the hatch puzzle and hopefully fool a trout or two. Start keeping a fishing diary not only to record fishing success, but also to detail hatches, water temperature, specific fishing techniques and successful fly patterns. You will be amazed at how quickly your information base builds and how valuable it becomes for planning future trips. And finally, remember to take time and just enjoy the outdoor experience. Your days on the water will be that much more rewarding.

Above: Rainbow trout tight to the lily pads.　　　　　*Photo: Brian Chan*

Right: Brian Chan contemplating a fly change.　　　　　*Photo: Harry Penner*

Below: Rainbow taken on a marabou leech pattern.　　　　*Photo: Brian Chan*

Aerial view of a typical interior lake shoal.   *Photo: Brian Chan*

Releasing a 20-inch rainbow trout.   *Photo: Brian Chan*

Opposite: Ice-off conditions prior to spring turnover is the "magic week." *Photo: Brian Chan*
Inset: Chrome-bright interior lake rainbow. *Photo: Brian Chan*

A.

B.

C.

D.

E.

F.

A. Darner dragonfly nymph
B. Traveling sedge larva
C. Damselfly nymph
D. Libellulid dragonfly nymph
E. *Gammarus* shrimp
F. *Callibaetis* mayfly nymph
G. Water boatman

Photos: Ron Boudreau

Opposite: Launching fly near the reeds.
Photo: Brian Chan

G.

52

Angler about to release a prime Kamloops trout. *Photo: Brian Chan*

Previous page: Belly boats and pontoon boats have become extremely popular when for searching out new lakes. *Photo: Harry Penner*

Winter and Summer Steelhead

by Art Lingren

Wow, what a fish!

Severely shaken by the rush of adrenaline as I knelt down to take the hook from the steelhead's mouth, those few words inadequately describe what had transpired over the previous few minutes. I love to fly fish for summer-run steelhead, and I love to bring the fish up to the surface to take a surface- or just-under-the-surface-presented fly. On this trip I had been at the fabled Dean River, located along B.C.'s central coast in Fisheries Management Region 5, for six days. Today I thought I would walk up to the Fir Pool. I couldn't leave the Dean without fishing the pool where I took my first summer-run steelhead fifteen seasons earlier. I had heard great changes had altered the pool, and although the changes to the Fir Pool were drastic, they didn't surprise me. I have wandered too many rivers over the past thirty-plus years and few, if any, have been unchanged by water flow—one of nature's most fascinating and powerful forces.

A large gravel bar had developed diagonally from the tail of the Fir to the bottom of the chute flowing from the upstream Grizzly Run. It looked wadeable. It was, and I could fish the classic fish-holding gut—a spot in a river that will stop a fish from migrating further upriver because of its depth and velocity—that had developed near the left bank. (The best spot turned out to be a little further downstream from where I started, but one should cover all likely looking water.

Sometimes you don't know what the water will fish like until you do a drift or two.) By methodically working the water I intended to work my way through the gut and was just enjoying being alive and on the Dean. I have caught steelhead from thirty-six of British Columbia's rivers through the years, but this day a fish took my Black Spey fly so violently and put up such a struggle, taking me well into my backing line, it had me scurrying over the rocks like never before. This thirty-three-inch male was truly one of the best fish I have ever caught. Perhaps the fish of a lifetime, but I will continue to cast my flies on steelhead waters hoping that someday a better fish will find my flies as attractive as this fish. Such are the dreams of steelhead fly fishers.

Steelhead Trout

What an unusual handle: steelhead. I have often wondered about the name's origin and spent nine months one year writing to museums and researching fisheries papers. Eventually I found early written records that showed steelhead and hardhead were the common names adopted by coastal market fishermen for this fish in the 1870s and perhaps earlier.

The steelhead is a seagoing rainbow trout. It spawns and offspring rear from one to three or four years in freshwater, depending on available food and growing season, before migrating to the ocean where they grow to a large size. When the steelhead returns to the river, it has a steely blue dorsal surface, silvery sides with black spots on its back, dorsal fin and tail. As it continues to mature after entering freshwater, it takes on the telltale coloration of its rainbow ancestors. Females, after months in freshwater, may only show a slight tinge of pink on the cheeks and have a light rainbow hue along the lateral line. Males color much more and more quickly. Steelhead return to fresh water to spawn after spending from a few months to three years ocean-feeding, and can range in size from about two pounds to more than thirty pounds. Although steelhead vary greatly in size, a five-pound steelhead is a small fish in British Columbia and any fish fifteen pounds and larger is a good-sized fish in most rivers.

Taking Times

When the steelhead makes its return to the river, it may hold near the mouth of the river until water conditions suit migration. On large rivers, like the Fraser and Skeena, that have large flows even at low levels, upstream migrations are not hampered. On some of the coastal rivers, the run is drawn in by an increase in flow, and on many rivers migration is instigated by the spring runoff.

Fast-running steelhead are poor "takers." However, a freshly arrived steelhead as it moves slowly up-river, stopping here and there to test the current, is an alert fish and can be a grand taker. Providing the angler matches his method to water conditions, the fish are relatively easy to catch. This is the time when inexperienced anglers often have good sport and experienced anglers have better sport.

After the run has arrived and the fish settle in, the fishing can vary from great to lousy, and success or failure is dependent on being there at the right time and the fish being undisturbed. On rivers popular with weekend fishers, Saturday can often be much better than Sunday. But, there are times after a run when water conditions change, and existing fish that have been difficult to catch suddenly become catchable again.

Size of Steelhead

Pacific Northwest steelhead vary in size: small ones weigh just three or four pounds, large ones are fifteen to twenty-five pounds, and huge ones are thirty pounds or greater. In the pre-catch-and-release days we killed the fish, and if we wanted to know how big it was we would weigh it before cleaning. Most steelhead rivers are catch-and-release on wild fish and many anglers measure the length, and sometimes the length and girth, of fish they release and try to approximate weights. Although it isn't scientifically sound, because girth dimensions play a large role in calculating accurate weights of fish released, I generally use the "length minus 20 rule" to come up with an approximate weight. The rule is a simple correlation between length and weight. To get an estimated weight for a 29-inch steelhead, subtract 20 inches and you come up with 9 lb. Simple, and this works for the average-girthed steelhead, plus or minus 10 percent, in the 25- to 35-inch range. By using this method we can quickly get an estimate of weight and get the fish back into the river for a speedy release. However, if your fish looks deep and/or is greater than thirty-five inches long and you want to determine a more accurate weight use Sturdy's formula. Weight in pounds = 0.00133 x (girth)^2 x length (girth and length in inches.) Following is a Sturdy weight chart for large fish.

Sturdy's formula for calculating weight of large fish:

LENGTH

		34	35	36	37	38	39	40	41	42	43	44	45	46
	16	11.6	11.9	12.3	12.6	12.9	13.3	13.6	14.0	14.3	14.6	15.0	15.3	15.7
	17	13.1	13.5	13.8	14.2	14.6	15.0	15.4	15.8	16.1	16.5	16.9	17.3	17.7
G	18	14.7	15.1	15.5	15.9	16.4	16.8	17.2	17.7	18.1	18.5	19.0	19.4	19.8
I	19	16.3	16.8	17.3	17.8	18.2	18.7	19.2	19.7	20.2	20.6	21.1	21.6	22.1
R	20	18.1	18.6	19.2	19.7	20.2	20.7	21.3	31.8	22.3	22.9	23.4	23.9	24.5
T														
H	21	19.9	20.5	21.1	21.7	22.3	22.9	23.5	24.0	24.6	25.2	25.8	26.4	27.0
	22	21.9	22.5	23.2	23.8	24.5	25.1	25.7	26.4	27.0	27.7	28.3	29.0	29.6
	23	23.9	24.6	25.3	26.0	26.7	27.4	28.1	28.8	29.5	30.3	31.0	31.7	32.4
	24	26.0	26.8	27.6	28.3	29.1	29.9	30.6	31.4	32.2	32.9	33.7	34.5	35.2
	25	28.3	29.1	29.9	30.8	31.6	32.4	33.3	34.1	34.9	35.7	36.6	37.4	38.2

For example, my friend, Van Egan, caught his largest-ever steelhead while fishing the Dean River in 1994 after nearly fifty years fly fishing for steelhead. The fish was very long at forty-three inches, but with a twenty-one-inch girth not a bulky, heavy fish for its length. From the summary table, to get the weight follow along the top, marked LENGTH, until you find 43 then go down the side, marked GIRTH, until you find 21 and you get 25.2 lb.

Steelhead populations vary from year to year and are small compared to salmon populations. For example, salmon populations occur in the thousands and tens of thousands with some sockeye and pink populations returning to their home rivers in the millions. Steelhead on the other hand generally number in hundreds with only a few stocks returning in the thousands. To illustrate, before incidental interceptions in the commercial and Native mixed stock fisheries, the Thompson River with three main stocks has a run of 6,000 to 10,000; the Skeena, with about five stocks, has 50,000 to 75,000; and the Chilliwack, with one stock, has a run of about 6,000 to 8,000.

In the mid-1980s we experienced the largest runs in recent years, perhaps larger than the runs of late 1960s and certainly larger than any in the 1970s. Steelhead returns and fishing all along the coast were phenomenal. However, like all cyclic things, the low must come and it is with us now. There is fear the low steelhead populations we now experience, because of decades of indiscriminate catches by market fishers, habitat destruction and the adverse effects of climate change on ocean survival, may not rebound. I hope not, but the warning signs are there. In past years, returns to the Thompson River in some seasons have neared the minimum number of 900 needed to sustain the stocks. East coast Vancouver Island streams have had closures due to poor returns during the 1997 and 1998 seasons.

Steelhead can be caught all year round in the province if you are willing to travel to different locations, and I have taken them in all months but June. Although they are morphologically the same fish, steelhead can be put into two racial groups: winter-run and summer-run. The characteristics that distinguish one race from the other are the timing of river entry and sexual maturity at entry. Summer-run steelhead enter fresh water often hundreds of kilometers from their destination stream through May to early October, and all summer-runs are sexually immature. Winter-run steelhead enter fresh water usually from December to May in a far more advanced state of sexual maturity than their summer-run counterparts, which do most of their maturing in the river during winter and spring. Both races spawn in the spring following their freshwater entry.

Winter-run

Around the beginning of winter, the first winter fish start to show in certain rivers. For example, the Yakoun River on the Queen Charlotte Islands has fish returning from November through May, the Cowichan on Vancouver Island and the Vedder in the Lower Mainland see returns from December through May. Peak timing of a run is dependent on many things, such as difficulty and length of the journey to the spawning grounds, and often on coastal rivers fish are drawn into the stream by the rains of winter. On some rivers like the Squamish or Wakeman, although they may have fish coming in as early as December, the bulk of the run is drawn in when the snow pack begins to melt, often in April or, if a late freshet, May. Those late-running winter fish are ready to spawn and do so quickly.

Winter steelhead fly fishing is tough. Water temperatures through most of the winter are around the 40°F range and often lower. Fish are not active takers in cold water. The fly fisher must go deep and dirty to be successful. To present the fly properly requires deep wading in cold water and even neoprene waders are often inadequate insulators. However, as winter wanes, usually in March, water temperatures start to move up and fish become more active. Even then the fly fisher needs to probe deeply with his flies. An angler will wonder when the fly stops on its swing whether it is bottom or a steelhead. Once the bottom moves, you won't know if it is a small steelhead or a twenty-pounder. No matter what size, any winter steelhead will leave you shaking with excitement as you play and land the fish. Fly fishers who work hard for winter fish will be rewarded.

Summer-run

Summer-run steelhead are interesting because they have the unique capability to access and use habitat not often available to their winter-returning cousins. These fish make the migration at just the right time. They are able to maximize their own upstream performance since their energy reserves are optimal for strength and endurance. They are not yet hindered by the physiological changes needed for spawning, which can be as long as nine or ten months away. The habitat they are seeking is often above tough canyon chutes and drops and they pick suitable water and river-temperature conditions as river runoff subsides. On small streams this can be as early as May, but on the larger waterways, such as the Fraser and Skeena, migration usually begins in late summer and continues through early fall. Anglers fishing world-renowned summer-run rivers such as the Thompson, Kispiox, Babine, Bulkley and Sustut catch steelhead during the late summer and fall through until the rivers close to angling on December 31. The fish they catch are summer-run steelhead. These fish entered fresh water in the summer and early fall months.

Steelhead are spring spawners and summer-runs return to the river with enough fat reserves to last them until the following spring and to endure the rigors of spawning. A small percentage of steelhead survive spawning, return to the sea and, after regeneration, return to spawn again.

The summer-run steelhead is a fly fisher's fish, especially during the summer and early fall months. Fly fishers will be fishing steelhead when water temperatures in the high 40° to 60°F range, optimum for fish activity. Summer-run steelhead are most active through those temperatures and will rise to take flies on or just below the surface. Whether the catch is a small twenty-incher or a huge fish of twenty pounds-plus, summer-run steelheaders can experience thrills beyond the wildest of dreams when one of those screamers grabs the fly.

River and Stream Tackle and Techniques

In river fishing, the range in fish size can be extreme and many anglers have outfits consisting of matching lines and rods ranging up to #11 to cover that diversity. On many of our steelhead rivers, the average fish may be eight to ten pounds, but most streams will have some fish in the fifteen- to twenty-pound range, with the occasional one even larger. In some rivers, such as the Thompson and Kispiox, fish between fifteen and twenty pounds are common and twenty-plus pounders are frequent. To satisfy my steelhead fly-fishing requirements, I generally use outfits in the #8 to #11 range.

I prefer river fishing to any other and have spent most of the past thirty years in pursuit of summer- and winter-run steelhead. Because of that preference I use special equipment and own three double-handed Spey rods of twelve, fifteen and seventeen and a half feet that throw lines varying from #8 to #11. However, such special tools are costly. If you do lake fishing and have a #7 outfit and are going to do a fair amount of river fishing for fish greater than ten pounds, you could cover most large-fish river fishing with a #9 single-handed outfit with the #7 still water being your back up. Casting a double-handed rod requires both hands, whereas a single-handed rod only requires one hand.

There are a large variety of lines ranging from full floaters, floaters with sink tips to full sinkers suitable for river fishing. A floating line is a must for presenting flies near or on the surface and for upstream sunk-fly fishing. I prefer to Spey cast—a technique developed by Atlantic salmon fisherman on the River Spey in Scotland—even with a single-handed rod, and I use a double-taper floating line instead of the now-popular weight forward. Nonetheless, the weight-forward lines are of good design, cast well and are preferred by many.

Most fish in rivers are bottom dwellers, and although some can be taken on flies on or near the surface, much of the time you must fish down to them. To accomplish this task, a fly fisher should have at least a couple of lines that sink—a fast sinker for slow-moving water and a superfast sinker for deeper and/or fast-moving water. Most fly fishers have abandoned the full sinkers for river fishing and go with sink tips. I make my own sink tips and have extrafast to slow-sink tips ranging from five to sixteen feet in length and loop them onto my double-taper #9, #10 or #11 floater for my steelhead fly fishing. For steelhead you must at times dredge the bottom and many fly fishers use one the Teeney T series of tips for their extrafast tip while others prefer a couple of sink tips from Cortland's or Scientific Anglers' series of lines. Big fish in flowing water usually require a larger capacity reel and a 100 to 200 yards of backing, depending on size of river and fish. Large steelhead on large rivers can use a lot of line.

Perhaps a few words about leaders is appropriate before I close on tackle and move onto steelhead flies. Fishing with a floating line requires a transfer of energy through the fly line and leader to the fly. A tapered leader helps transfer the energy and present the fly properly. However, you don't need costly tapered leaders for sunk-line fishing. For sunk-line, you attach directly to the end of your sink tip or full-sinking line a three- or four-foot section of ten- to fifteen-pound tippet material.

Most steelhead that are catchable will be in three to six feet of water and the purpose of fishing a sunk line is to get the fly down to proper fishing depth quickly. On fast-flowing rivers, if you use a nine- to twelve-foot tapered leader, often your drift is complete by the time the fly has had a chance to sink very deep. By using a short leader attached directly to the fly line, the fly will sink with the line and be down to maximum fishing depth, resulting in a better drift and presentation. Some fly fishers dress their flies with lead and others attach a small split shot to make sure the fly sinks quickly. Flies with lead included in their dressing is permissible on fly-fishing-only waters, but adding external weight to the line is against regulations.

Flies

There are hundreds of steelhead patterns from which a fly fisher can choose, and each locale will have its favorites. One pitfall that distracts many anglers is the change-fly syndrome. This occurs when the fly fishers have so many flies with no criteria for matching conditions with technique they are constantly changing patterns in search of the magic fly. Through many years fishing many rivers, I have surmised that an experienced fly fisher using sound judgment needs only five basic patterns. With a variety of sizes in those basic patterns and if the fisher is able to marry size and pattern to water and light conditions and presentation techniques he or she will spend more productive time fishing.

The five basic patterns include a large fly, such as the General Practitioner, for colored- and/or cold-water conditions, and for use in poor light. It is often, but not exclusively, used on a sunk line. A short-bodied, quick-sinking pattern, such as the Cowichan Coachman, is for use in upstream, sunk fly (nymphtype) presentations. A slim-bodied pattern, such as the Black Spey, is useful for floating-line fishing. A clipped deer hair fly, such as the famous Bomber, is handy for skating across the surface using a floating line and one should have a fly, such as Roderick Haig-Brown's Steelhead Bee, for dry fly fishing. A fly fisher can substitute many patterns for any suggested above as long as the pattern suits the technique. For example, a Woolly Bugger, Egg Sucking Leech or Taylor's Golden Spey will do for the General Practitioner. I prefer the GP because the tail and hackle move enticingly and add life as it sweeps through the current, but if you fancy something less lifelike, the Squamish Poacher is a favorite of many. It certainly sinks quickly. A Woolly Worm can be substituted for the Cowichan Special, a slim-bodied sparsely dressed skunk, Doc Spratley, Purple Peril, or as specified for the Black Spey, a Combo Bug, Lemire's Irresistible, Tom Thumb or Greaseliner for the Bomber, and a Tom Thumb, Grey Wulff or Royal Coachman for the Steelhead Bee.

The Sunk-line Presentation

Most salmonids when observed in their river environment will be seen close to the bottom. And it is this observation, made hundreds of years ago, that has prompted man to fish down to them. Fishing the sunk fly on a down and across sweep with a General Practitioner or substitute is a favorite technique of many fly fishers and one of the most effective ways of catching steelhead with a fly. Before casting the fly, the fisher needs to examine the velocity of the water and configuration of the pool—called reading the water—and then select the best angle for the cast. Usually the cast is about 30° to 60° downstream of the angler and brought across the current and ends up directly below and close to the shore.

Many rivers can be fished effectively with a single-handed rod using the sunk-line technique and it is a favored tool on the smaller rivers. But with the reintroduction of the double-handed fly-rod in the early 1980s, fly fishermen who used it properly, now had a tool that would permit them to cover as much as ninety feet of water with good line control, compared to the fifty or sixty feet of control that single-handed rods permitted.

Accompanying the reintroduction of the two-fisted rods in British Columbia was Spey casting and the double-taper fly line. Not only did this casting technique suit the floating-line presentation, but because of improved line control it made the presentation of the sunk-fly more effective. In 1984, after I became adept at Spey casting, I thought that I could present the fly better, and fish the sunk-fly with more control by looping a section of sinking line onto the end of my double-taper floating line. The results were startling. Spey casts of eighty feet or better were the norm, and on the first day I tried this combination up on the Dean River, six fish took the fly.

The sunk-line is the tool to use when the river is cold and the fish lethargic, or the river is colored and you need to get the fly down to the fish. However, because of changing river velocity, you need to choose a sink-tip that suits the water speed.

Indeed, I remember a couple of days when I used the sunk-line technique with rather surprising results. I had driven to the Thompson River with a couple of friends one day late in November. With just more than two hours of daylight remaining in the day I decided to fish the sunk-line and looped on a seven-foot high-speed, high-density sink tip onto the end of my double-taper #11 floating fly-line. In the next two-and-a-half hours I beached a fine brace of Thompson River steelhead—one 36 fi-inch male and a 35-inch female. Expectations at the start of the day often don't match the results at the end of the day, and I was more than happy with two fish in such short time. You wonder as the day ends what tomorrow holds.

The next day proved better than the afternoon before. Indeed it was, in the first twelve minutes of fishing I had three takes, losing one fish and landing a 34-inch female. Then after lunch, in the next pool, in forty-five minutes fishing with the same combination—Black GP fly and 7-foot sink tip—I landed a brace of 37-inch males. What a day—five takes, one fish lost and three landed.

The down and across presentation used for fishing the sunk-line also suits the floating line technique.

The Floating Line

In the history of fly fishing, this is a relatively new method. It is a very pleasant way to fish for steelhead. It has been called greased-line, floating-line and dry-line fishing. The correct name for it is floating-line fishing. The purpose is to present a fly close to the surface with a line that floats on the surface. This method found its way across the Atlantic to the West Coast in the 1930s when Rod Haig-Brown and General Noel Money used it in the later 1930s for Stamp River summer-run steelhead. Haig-Brown first wrote about it in *The Western Angler* (1939), and the method has had devotees since that time.

Indeed, I remember when I decided to fly fish the Thompson River. I had heard the water suited the floating-line technique and that is what I used. On a sunny, windy October afternoon I started in on the lower part of the Graveyard Run and worked my way downstream to the rock island. There is a slick at the top end of this water, and I cast my Doc Spratley out and let it come around when I felt what I thought to be a good trout take the fly. It didn't get hooked. My next cast sent my fly through the same water again, I know a fish grabbed it, but all I remember was having my line ripped from the reel and a Thompson steelhead jumping halfway across the river. Gently, I played the fish, and proud I was of the thirty-four-inch female that I landed. Early success brings confidence, and that early Thompson success with the floating line made me a devotee of the technique.

In summer-run streams, like the Dean River, even under optimum water temperatures, because of colored water conditions it is often necessary to use the sunk-line to catch steelhead. However many steelhead streams are almost always clear. With clear-water conditions it is water temperature and depth that dictate fly presentation. A fly fisher must be receptive to use the floating-line technique when clear and warm water conditions prevail. Confidence in method, fly and your own skill is vital for success, and confidence in the floating-line technique will bring rewards. Indeed, fishing the floating line with a slim-bodied fly can be very profitable in water conditions that suit the method.

The Skated or Waked Fly

This is the last of the fly-fishing methods where the fly is cast out either opposite or below the fisher and is brought down and across the current. With both sunk-line and floating-line presentations, the fly is below the surface of the water, but with the skated fly it is not. The main intent of this presentation is to skate a fly over the lie.

This is an old technique dating back to seventeenth-century Britain. The waked or skated fly presentation has had, over the years, many names attached to it. Dibbling, skimming, skittering, waking, riffling, dry-fly fishing and surface-lure are some names that come to mind. All, except dry-fly fishing, are proper terms used to describe the method in which the fly is brought across the surface of water causing a wake. I can't emphasize enough that it is the fly that attracts the attention of the fish, and often a half hitch (the leader looped around the eye so it comes off the side) back of the hook eye ensures the fly will wake even in the calmest of waters.

The waked-fly technique is less consistent than the floating- and sunk-line techniques. You need optimum light conditions with alert fish in water of suitable depth and temperature. However, if you decide to use only this method, you have to fish it at those times of the day when the poorer light conditions exist and, on those bright, sunlit days, using the waked-fly method can severely limit your fishing day.

Although it is perhaps a less productive method, the waked-fly presentation does bring some spectacular rises. Unfortunately, many are false rises, and misses are common when using this technique. To the fish, the dominant target is the apex of the V at the end of the hook, and that is what the fish keys in on. And of course, when it goes after the apex, we end up with a flashy, exciting rise and no hook-up because the fish missed the hook. I remember one evening on the Dean River when I had ten rises to a skated fly with the fly getting the mouth of only three fish: I pricked one, lost one and landed one. You can't catch a fish unless you get it to take the fly into its mouth. Nonetheless, if employed wisely, a Bomber used with the skated-fly technique does bring some of the best thrills there are in steelhead fly fishing. And it does get the attention of traveling fish (some large fish at that). Some fishers I know will fish the waked fly, but when they get a couple of showy rises they will change to a sparsely dressed fly of the right size fished on the floating line and catch the fish.

The waked-fly presentation has become a popular way of fly fishing on many summer-run steelhead streams, and, under the right light and water conditions, it can be effective. One of the reasons it's popular is because all can be seen and because of that it is one of the easiest to learn. However, no matter how exciting the rises, the waked-fly technique will never replace the two more skilled presentation methods of down-and-across fly fishing—the floating and sunk line. All three of these presentations—floating line, sunk line and waked fly—are useful methods, when employed under proper conditions, for covering and searching steelhead water.

Dry Fly

The last two methods—dry fly and upstream sunk fly—suit the single-handed rod, upstream approach to known fish-holding spots and both techniques are more suitable for pools that hold fish for a period.

Although steelhead respond probably much more readily to the waked fly over the dry fly, many steelhead fly fishers do not make a distinction between the waked fly and the dry fly. I do. I have too deep a respect for the British fly fishing roots and masters that preceded me to disregard the work of anglers such as George LaBranche, E. R. Hewitt and especially Roderick Haig-Brown who promoted the dry-fly technique more than any other steelhead fly fisher.

Dry flies were introduced to B.C. about seventy-five years ago on the Capilano River and had followers on that river until construction of the Cleveland Dam in 1954 drowned favored runs. Rod Haig-Brown revitalized the fly in the 1950s and 1960s on the Campbell and Heber rivers and he wrote about that technique in *Fisherman's Summer* (1959) and *Fisherman's Fall* (1964).

John Fennelly's *Steelhead Paradise* is an account of his adventures fly fishing for steelhead in the Skeena watershed and he describes the dry-fly technique well: "When I fish for steelhead with a dry fly, I use exactly the same technique that I would in casting for any other type of trout. I try to get into position about twenty feet below the fish and well off to one side. I then use a 'slack line' or 'curve' cast so as to permit as long a free drift of the fly as possible" (p. 73).

Haig-Brown, who wrote about taking steelhead on dries as early as 1951, and Fennelly, years later, describe similar dry-fly techniques and both realized that fish often came to the fly once it ended its drift and started to wake. In fact a dragged fly often moved fish that were unmovable to the drifted fly. Steelhead fly fishers were quick to adapt and ended up with the down-and-across fly presentation described earlier as the waked-fly technique. The traditional dry-fly technique developed by LaBranche and Hewitt for Atlantic salmon and Haig-Brown for steelhead requires the fly to float drag free.

Upstream Sunk Fly

This is another technique that favors an upstream presentation to fish in known holding waters and is more suitable to the single-handed rod. This technique often works well when fish have been in a pool for a while and won't respond because they are stale or spooky, or the water has cooled and they won't rise. Often steelhead are found in deep holding pools and this is the only technique, using a weighted fly such as a Cowichan Special, to get down to the bottom-hugging fish. Usually a weighted fly is cast above the holding spot and allowed to sink down to the level of the fish so it does not have to move much to take the fly.

To Sum Up

Indeed, opportunities exist on Northwest steelhead streams to use all five techniques and variations of those techniques described in this discourse. However, combining the correct fly pattern with presentation and water and light conditions are critical for consistent success on any steelhead river. The following table provides some guidelines on marrying water temperature and clarity, light conditions, technique and pattern. However, nothing in fly fishing is absolute —this is only a guide, but it will get you started on the right track.

Conditions and Techniques

WATER (°F)	RIVER TYPE	TECHNIQUE	FLY TYPE
Less than 48°	1. Run 2. Pocket	1. Sunk-line 2. Upstream-sunk	1. GP-type 2. Nymph-type

Comments
The colder the water the slower and closer to the fish the fly needs to be presented. The floating-line technique can be effective in the high 40°s.

WATER (°F)	RIVER TYPE	TECHNIQUE	FLY TYPE
48° to 55°	1. Run 2. Run 3. Run 4. Pocket	1. Sunk-line 2. Floating-line 3. Skated-fly 4. Upstream-sunk	1. GP-type 2. to 8s sparse 3. Bomber-type 4. Nymph-type

Comments
1. If water visibility is poor use the sunk-line all day.
2. Use larger fly in lower temperatures. Using a floating line with sparsely dressed fly can be the only effective way of catching steelhead during the midday light.
3. Nymph-type presentation can be very effective for seen fish that have settled in, i.e., stale fish.

WATER (°F)	RIVER TYPE	TECHNIQUE	FLY TYPE
55° to 65°	1. Run 2. Run 3. Run 4. Pocket 5. Pocket	1. Sunk-line 2. Floating-line 3. Skated-fly 4. Upstream-sunk 5. Dry-fly	1. GP-type 2. sparse 2 to 8s 3. Bomber-type 4. Nymph-type 5. Steelhead Bee-type

Comments
1. If water visibility is poor, use the sunk-line all day.
2. Use larger floating-line type fly in lower temperatures. Floating-line can be the only effective way of catching steelhead during the midday light on sun-baked runs. Large GP-type fly can be effective fished with a floating line in poor light conditions such as those found during the early morning, late evening or on overcast days.
3. Skated presentation is effective during poor light conditions or on shaded portions of run. It is not effective during the heat of the day on sun-baked runs.
4. Nymph-type presentation can be very effective with stale fish in known holding spots.
5. The natural drift dry fly is best tried at the higher temperature regimes.

Above: Anglers flyfishing the Graveyard Run on the Thompson River.   *Photo: Harry Penner*

Left: A Thompson River summer-run steelhead.   *Photo: Harry Penner*

Below: Author with one on!   *Photo: Art Lingren*

Previous page: A classic Vancouver Island steelhead run.   *Photo: Art Lingren*

Art Lingren with a 36-inch male.

Photo: Art Lingren

This 33-inch steelhead took a Black Spey on a floating line.

Photo: Art Lingren

Above: Mark Pendlington fly fishing the Thompson River for summer-run steelhead.

Photo: Art Lingren

Left: Angler Spey casting on the Thompson River. These two-handed rods have become very popular on steelhead rivers.

Photo: Harry Penner

Left: Arthur Lingren with a 35-inch male steelhead. *Photo: Art Lingren*

Below: Arthur Lingren about to launch a fly on the Dean River. *Photo: Art Lingren*

Arthur Lingren fly fishing a run on the Stamp River for winter steelhead.   *Photos: Harry Penner*

Winter steelheading on the Cowichan. Winter steelheading is a tough proposition but rewards come to those who make an effort. *Photo: Art Lingren*

Saltwater Fly Fishing for Salmon

by Barry M. Thornton

Saltwater fly fishing for Pacific salmon along the West Coast is still in a pioneer state. That it has not received prior acclaim and acquired an active following is likely because earlier sport boats did not provide the wide-searching hunting capability necessary to locate feeding salmon schools. As well, fly lines were not able to quick-sink to the magic salmon striking zones of twenty to forty feet. However, since the resource has now been recognized as finite and fly fishers are abandoning historic fly fishing constraints for new concepts, such as sleek silver flies, anchoring in the ocean, slow-strip retrieves and catch and release, a new ocean fly fishery has evolved. Those who have been fortunate enough to have experienced the locomotive run of the king of Pacific salmon, the chinook; the water ballet of the prince of Pacific salmon, the coho; or the powerful dogged head shake of the princess of Pacific salmon, the pink, are addicted to a lifelong search for open-water salmon. For those who have not tried this developing fishery, there are almost infinite numbers of locations on the Pacific Northwest coast waiting for the adventurous fly fisher.

The Northwest coast is a vast area with thousands of miles of shoreline and many offshore islands. Mile-high coastal mountains funnel the region's thousands of rivers, streams and creeks into small estuaries all along many lengthy, deep fiords. Each of these numerous waterways provides natal watersheds, the nurseries for five separate Pacific salmon species. Three of these species, coho, chinook and pink, are the traditional primary targets of the West Coast fly fisher while the other two, sockeye and chum, are only now becoming recognized as another potential fly fishery.

Pacific Salmon

Pacific salmon are large, powerful sports fish with a unique life history and cycle. A basic knowledge of the five species is helpful for the fly fisher and provides an understanding of when and where to best locate these mighty fish.

Chinook salmon (*Oncorhynchus tshawytscha*) are the kings of all the Pacific salmon. Other common names include spring, jack spring, winter spring, smiley (a commercial term for fish more than twelve pounds) and tyee (the name used for all chinook weighing more than thirty pounds). Chinook inhabit all major river systems along the B.C. coast and are common in many smaller streams. It is a salmon that hugs the coastline during its ocean travels, making it available all along the coast for the fly fisher. Because of its long stay in the ocean, from one to seven years, it also remains in some areas all months of the year. Spawning runs usually begin in August, although some chinook will enter their natal river in June.

Coho salmon (*Oncorhynchus kisutch*) are the princes of the Pacific salmon. Other common names include silver, blueback (a regional term for coho weighing less than five pounds) and northerns (a reference for migrating coho, usually late summer, with a well-developed kype). Coho also inhabit all major river systems, most streams and many creeks. Coho bluebacks begin to show in surface schools along coastal areas in February. Fly fishing is possible in the open ocean because they are near the surface. They grow rapidly feeding on euphasiids (pink feed). Sometime in May they change their diet to feed on baitfish. This rich protein accounts for their rapid growth during the summer months. The spawning run begins in October in most rivers, but they also move along beaches and estuaries where they are exciting targets for the beach fly fisher.

Pink salmon (*Oncorhynchus gorbuscha*) are the princesses of the Pacific salmon. Other common names include humpy, which is a reference to the large dorsal hump on mature males. Pinks have a two-year life cycle which results in them being smaller than other salmon. They begin to show in large numbers along the inner B.C. coast in July. They are found in schools along the beaches near their home estuaries, a prime location for the beach fly fisher.

Sockeye salmon (*Oncorhynchus nerka*) have recently become a primary target for the ocean fly fisher in areas where they concentrate prior to their journey up their natal river. Other common names include red salmon, which is a reference to the deep red skin of the fish that have reached the spawning grounds. Their spawning runs become available in June through August.

Chum salmon (*Oncorhynchus keta*) have also only recently become a target salmon in river estuary zones. Other common names include dog salmon, referring to the long teeth on the kype of spawning fish, and calico salmon because of the purple, blue and yellow splotched sides of mature spawning fish. Chum are a late arriving salmon, entering their home rivers in November.

Estuary and Feeder Salmon

For the fly fisher targeting Pacific salmon, it is important to distinguish between the two saltwater phases of the salmon's life cycle. Each phase occurs during a particular period in the salmon's life odyssey and requires a much different fly angling approach.

The first and most common phase is that of concentrations of estuary salmon. Estuary salmon are akin to river salmon for they have become inhibited through a natural anorexia state and cease feeding. As well, they are completely overcome by a homing instinct and a need to spawn. In this phase, Pacific salmon, whether they are coho, chinook, pink, chum or sockeye, are best fished with an attractor streamer fly featuring silver and, if necessary, one other color like blue, pink, red or orange.

The second phase concentrates on feeder salmon. These are the schooling salmon located throughout inshore Pacific Coast saltwater that go through voracious feeding frenzies. These feeder salmon are sought after in a searching fashion as opposed to estuary salmon, which are relatively easy to locate at the mouth of rivers. In fact, most estuary salmon are more successfully fly fished by wading in beach shallows at varying tide stages rather than from a boat.

It has been with fly patterns that I have found the greatest difference between feeder and estuary salmon. Feeder salmon prefer sleek, slender, silver patterns that are an obvious imitation of baitfish—and I mean sleek, slender and silver. I have on occasion even used a single stainless steel hook with a small streamer of white polar bear hair for saltwater fly fishing and have regularly hooked coho and chinook salmon.

Be careful with color in your patterns! Color both entices and spooks feeder salmon. Pink or fluorescent lime green (chartreuse) seems to attract coho and chinook in some situations, but nothing works as effectively as silver. I have one fly which I have perfected over the years—the Silver Thorn. It now has more than twenty-eight variations, all having hooked coho and chinook in numerous situations. The primary materials, stainless steel hooks and silver tinsel chenille, can be combined with many other materials in an almost infinite variety of patterns for this most-effective saltwater salmon fly.

Estuary salmon, on the other hand, need an attractor streamer fly. Patterns can vary from the Mickey Fin to the Pink Eve. They too seem to require a silver body, but here color becomes much more important. My most effective pattern over the years has been the Pink Eve, a pattern that works equally well for estuary pink and coho salmon.

One important fly fisher attitude change is necessary for effective open water salmon fly fishing for both estuary and feeder salmon. For decades fly fishers have lived with the knowledge that bucktailing a fly behind the boat at fast speeds is effective for hooking salmon (and other fish). But fly fishers need to realize they can neither retrieve their fly at the speed required for bucktailing nor cover the area required when bucktailing. (Bucktailing is simply that method of trolling a bare fly at varying distances and speeds behind the boat.) Fortunately, a slow-stripped fly in hook sizes #6 to #2/0 does attract salmon. Salmon strikes on a slow-strip retrieve are rarely smash strikes. In fact most of these strikes, while emphatic, consist only of a sudden halt and a slow give. Coho are notorious for this sudden halt, and, in many situations, they will actually come toward the boat and near the surface with an open mouth. But when they realize they have been hooked it is time to clear the fly line of snags and wait for that water-walking outburst!

Hunting for Salmon

In my book, *Saltwater Fly Fishing for Pacific Salmon* (Hancock House Publishers), I spend a great deal of time discussing hunting for salmon. This is the skill of reading the numerous saltwater environmental conditions that lead to successful saltwater salmon fly fishing. Nature's signals are many when you are on the open ocean. Some are displayed almost as vividly as flashing neon billboards to guide hunting fly fishers to prime locations. Some signs, such as specific hovering and flying gull species, compact baitfish schools and salmon surface activity, should never be ignored. They add much to the fishing experience and can be counted upon to target precise locations for the salmon fly fisher. One good example of their importance occurred of a recent trip.

I had left the boat launch at midmorning expecting to find coho in a location south of one of the Gulf Islands. I had received numerous reports of good catches in that area all week and, armed with this encouraging information, I planned to locate in a shallows where I knew the coho and chinook fed. But, to my surprise, when I arrived, I spotted family groups of sea ducks—loons, auks and murrelets—calmly swimming back to the beach. I was too late. The bite was off!

Had these sea ducks been swimming out from shore or compacted in tight surface flocks I would have known there were feeding salmon in the area. I was so dismayed that I almost suggested that we head back to the dock. However my sources had told me of fish in the area so we began a zigzagging, binocular searching hunt around the island. I have found it is possible there will be feeding salmon in one area, even if the bite is off in another.

Our first sign of potential activity occurred a few miles away on the east side of the island. Here we spotted concentrations of larger herring gulls. Both the white adults and the gray yearlings were congregating a few hundred yards offshore. When we boated over to the spots we drew out our fly rods in preparation to drift with the first herring ball, but stopped when we saw the dorsal fin and top-heavy tail of circling Pacific dogfish. There would be no salmon here, for we knew salmon and dogfish rarely mingle.

I drove the boat to a section of kelp that appeared to have a feeding flock of about a dozen Bonaparte's gulls. Just at the drop-off end of the kelp, I was astounded to read on my depth sounder a thick carpet of young herring in about twenty feet of water. I could just feel the fighting salmon in this fishy area. Anchoring the boat, we began our casting, letting the wet fly lines sink near the bottom. Then, with slow-strip retrieves, we began our fishing. The first coho came after only a few casts, a fish that we could actually see take the Silver Thorn pattern, darting out from a school of five coho. This was one of those exciting days when we had found active salmon after taking the time to follow a variety of nature's signals.

Once you have read these beacons, it is vital that you put your casting skills to work.

Anchoring to Cast

In the ocean, the water is never still! To counter this constant movement it is necessary that you anchor. To many fishers, anchoring in saltwater to fly fish for Pacific salmon seems to be a strange concept. I am not certain why. Possibly it has to do with the fact that salmon are always on the move and a successful salmon fisher has always appeared to be someone who is continually traveling from one location to another trolling or drift fishing. Maybe because the size and depth of the ocean are so vast, anchoring seems to be a restriction that would certainly limit success. Whatever the reason, many fly fishers seem to have difficulty with the idea.

I have found fruitful anchoring locations require a number of factors occur on that specific day at that specific time. These elements usually include tide movement, a concentration of baitfish, an active feeding school of salmon and structure in the form of kelp beds and/or specific underwater land forms.

Why anchor? The two reasons I have found most essential for salmon fly fishing success center around location and equipment. Firstly, anchoring gives you the opportunity to sink and control your fly line. Modern fly fishing lines are now capable of sinking quickly to salmon's preferred depths of fifteen to forty feet. Heavy-grained fly lines, those higher than 500 grains, are available to cast with matching rods as high as ASA (American Sporting Association rating) #12–if your arm will take it. As well, there is the alternate system of five- to thirty-foot shooting heads which can be loop-attached to fast full-sinking wet lines in a standard ASA #8 fly rod. This latter unit of tackle is the one I prefer because I recognize my own limitation with extraheavy equipment. When I happen to hook a smiley I simply let them run, for I always spool extra backing on my reel.

It is critical that you get down to the salmon feeding depths. I have found that it is the rare salmon that will come up for my fly. If you do not anchor and mend your fly line after the cast (yes, mend your line just like river fly fishing), the tidal currents and the ebbs and flows in the various thermoclines will quickly stretch your fly line out. This results in the line being lifted toward the surface. Therefore, this is one of the fundamental reasons for anchoring!

The second primary reason for anchoring is to retain location. Those who have fished the ocean know that tidal flows and wind will drift you past the salmon feeding hot spot far too quickly. When salmon fly fishing, choosing a location involves a precise combination of many factors. First, there must be baitfish in the vicinity. Second, the depth must be reasonable for fly lines to reach the salmon feeding depths, and third, there must be structure.

Structure can take the form of a single object like a kelp bed or an underwater pinnacle, or structure may result from a combination of items. To comprehend structure for salmon fly fishing it is important to understand the salmon's feeding behavior. For the purposes of this discussion I am going to concentrate on two Pacific salmon species, the chinook and coho, and look at prespawning summer behavior during the active feeding months of late June, July and August. These are the two most desired sport species and their principle fishing seasons. Each of the five Pacific salmon species has specific behavioral feeding patterns that need to be addressed separately. Fortunately for the fly fisher, chinook and coho have many feeding similarities; they can be fished in a similar manner; and they are often caught together in the same locations.

On the Pacific Northwest coast, coho and chinook migrate close to the shore during their homeward summer southern migration. When they are not feeding, both species seek deep waters for safety and security. These are often very deep waters ranging from 150 to 300 feet, or deeper if the coastal shelf allows it. At these extreme depths it is impossible to reach these fish during nonfeeding times with conventional fly lines. Even if you could, it would be rare for a salmon to take your fly for they are simply not in a feeding mood. But, when the feeding urge occurs, coho and chinook follow what I like to call "fish trails" to the feeding grounds. These fish trails are like their counterpart on land, the game trails that wildlife use. Traveling from their resting thermocline, salmon follow the topography of the underwater land, whether a sandy incline, a rising ravine or a sheer cliff, upward out of the depths to the open, shallow "baitfish meadows" where herring, needlefish and other prey fish concentrate.

These fish trails are special places for the fly fisher. When they have been defined and located, they are classic locations to anchor and intercept salmon venturing forth to the baitfish meadows. Because salmon migrate as a school, fishing will be hot one day then gone the next. But if you are fortunate to be at one of these baitfish meadows when coho and chinook pause in their southern migration, it is possible to have a number of successive days of incredible fly fishing.

Anchoring will greatly increase your opportunities on these feeding grounds, but like the predatory salmon, you too must prepare for opportunistic fly fishing when the baitfish move. Preying salmon tend to concentrate baitfish near kelp beds. Salmon seem to be reluctant to prey upon baitfish in the kelp and instead will hunt on the outskirts of the compacted schools of baitfish. Their constant harassment will move schools of baitfish along the kelp beds concentrating them in ever-changing locations. Success for the fly fisher is greatest when you are able to cast in such a manner that your fly is slow-stripped back into the baitfish as they compact when the preying salmon are near. This prime location changes with the travel of baitfish and requires a continual hoisting of your anchor so that you can move with the baitfish school. The only time I have found that this does not matter is when you are able to anchor at the deep end of a kelp bed, a kelp corner or sheer drop-off where the baitfish remain constant. This is an angling experience factor that takes time to learn, but once you have found such a location it should become a primary anchoring location when there are salmon in the area.

Opportunistic anchoring also occurs in shallow beach areas where baitfish have been forced to concentrate near the shore. These particular areas are usually quite dramatic because one is able to see thick carpets of baitfish and surface-slashing coho or chinook. The preying salmon move the bait-fish along the shore and often trap them in small bays or against exposed large boulders (see the anecdote at chapter's end for an example of this occurrence). On rare occasions I have watched coho actually beach themselves and then flop back into the sea during their furious attacks on baitfish. I have even seen them jump over exposed boulders in frothed attacks on their panic-stricken prey. Naturally, the ferocity of their attacks pushes the baitfish along the beach. I have found it necessary in these situations to hoist anchor and follow so that I can place my fly near the action. But because these bait-fish patches move up and down the beach, on occasion I have remained in one location and have found that traveling salmon will take my fly, even as it dapples unattended out the back of the boat, usually while I am pouring a needed cup of coffee. This happened to me twice one day at one of these beach locations! Be prepared for the hot mug-up!

A third primary anchoring location is near structure in sandy flats. Assuming there are baitfish in the vicinity, any structure that provides possible safety, such as a rising pinnacle or glacial boulder, is a location where these baitfish will concentrate when there are predator salmon in the area. I like to locate these underwater structures after I have found nearby baitfish schools and then anchor on the shallowest top of the structure. Once anchored, I cast outward so that my fly reaches beyond the structure and is stripped up along the incline of the structure where the baitfish congregate.

A fourth and very successful anchoring location is near the head of salmon fish trails. Often these locations are obvious for they are the fishing holes where all salmon sport anglers concentrate. On most summer days, sports boats can be found concentrated around some island, bay or landform. These are locations that have baitfish concentrations and underwater structures that concentrate salmon. It is important to find the precise location that intercepts the feeding salmon as they travel up out of the depths to the baitfish meadow.

Anchoring for salmon is one of those angling concepts that comes with experience. On the rare occasion your arm will ache from the intensive battles you have with these powerful sports fish. But, on most trips, the salmon will only come after much casting, and often when they are least expected. I have found that if the salmon are there, and if they are feeding, success is inevitable. Fly fishing in salt waters for salmon is a new challenge. All it requires is concentration, confidence, commitment and a carefully placed anchor.

Five Key Anchoring Tips

1. Tie your anchor rope on a side rail near the center of the boat. The constant wind on the open ocean always pushes your boat away from the anchor. If you tie the rope at the side, you increase your effective fishing zone because you are fishing right at the rail.

2. Use a hollow cement block as an anchor. I have used many anchors in my search for salmon and prefer the hollow cement block for boats up to twenty feet in length. The hollow block ties easily on your anchor rope, and if the anchor is eased into the water sensibly it rarely breaks. Because of its shape, it catches well on rock or sandstone bottoms. It also catches well in kelp forests and can be lifted quite easily. If necessary on sandy bottoms, two blocks can be used quite effectively on separate anchor ropes.

3. Make use of small floats to help triangulate a prime location. GPS (Global Position Satellite System) locators are now capable of taking you back to precise known locations. But a depth sounder is still a necessary tool to locate key underwater structure and baitfish.

4. Have a dry line outfit ready at all times to cast to surfacing salmon. Being prepared with a dry line or short sink tip (5 to 10 ft.) has resulted in many salmon for me. In an active anchoring area I have this outfit ready with line stripped out and sitting in a fish bucket (stripping basket) for those active salmon feeders that have surfaced. I have always been amazed at how often a salmon will take my fly when I cast to the "window" area where I have seen a feeding surfacing fish. The window is the conical area that the salmon can see on the surface.

5. On your anchor rope tie a quick release snap so that you can chase those tyee that never seem to stop running. These chinook salmon are so large and so powerful, it is almost impossible to fight them from an anchored boat. They must be chased. I use a simple brass clip with a small float attached so that I am able to quickly throw my anchor rope overboard knowing I can return to the visible float after the fight with a salmon.

Beach Fly Fishing for Pacific Salmon

"Here they come! Here they come!" This is the beach salmon fly fisher's call. It resounds along Pacific Coast beaches, carried on the crests of incoming waves echoed by fly anglers on extended solitary shorelines. Wind, tides and seabirds all add their excited reverberating clamor, creating that remarkable experience that is salmon saltwater beach fly fishing. This call begins in late July with the arrival of the first runs of pink salmon and extends through to November as chinook, coho, then chum swim the beaches near their home estuary.

One of the most alluring aspects of beach salmon fly fishing is that it is easily accessible to all fly fishers—young or old, experienced or novice. On the coast of British Columbia the beach areas where these salmon gather are often wide expanses of sand or cobblestone rocks. Foot access is usually possible from numerous locations. Once on the beach, the fly fisher has miles of open intertidal estuary and foreshore to hike and hunt for those compact schools of returning salmon. Once a school of salmon is located, usually by the obvious leaping silver "locator fish," it is possible for the fly fisher to position himself to intercept that traveling school.

For those fly fishers who are new to saltwater beach fly fishing there are some specific factors which should be considered: tides and currents, wind and cold, and salt, salt, salt.

In the Pacific Northwest, tides change about once every six hours. Every day there is an extreme low and an extreme high tide, with the difference between these extremes often reaching fifteen feet. It is imperative the fly fisher has a current tidal chart for the waters where he is fishing. These guides are always available at local sporting stores.

Pink and coho salmon travel up and down beach areas near their home estuary area at any tide level. On some tides (high, low, slack, ebb or flood) they appear to be closer to the shore than others, but this can change each day. Safety for the fly fisher must be considered every time you venture on the beach. During a low tide there usually is easy access to beach bays and flats, but be careful during the flood that you are continually moving back up the beach to the high tide line so that you are not trapped on innocent shoals or flats.

Ocean currents are another factor and, combined with tides, they can often become quite forceful, some to the extent that you feel like you are standing in a fast-moving river. These currents vary with every beach and should be considered each time you are wading. Ocean currents will occur during slack periods as well as at flood or ebb periods. On the West Coast cobblestone beaches it is often difficult to maintain a firm footing, therefore care should be taken to ensure the currents are not too strong.

On most beaches, pink salmon move close to the shore tasting the unmixed fresh river water which has not yet been stirred with the saltwater. Tidal currents keep this fresh water on the surface and close to shore and these are what draw the pinks close. Coho salmon on the other hand tend to stay further out.

A coastal summer does not always mean shirt-sleeve weather! Wear a wide-brim hat for protection from the bright sun and insulated waders for protection from the cold ocean waters. Winds are common at this time of the year; the breezes flow down the many fiords from snowcapped mountains and across the cool waters. A light windbreaker is a must.

Salt can be the ocean beach fly fisher's nemesis! But if a few precautions are taken it will not hinder your fishing. It goes without saying that fly reels, unless they are corrosive resistant, and lines should be thoroughly washed in fresh water after each trip on the ocean. This is a must! The fly fisher should also go on the water with a package of band-aides or a stripping finger guard that should be placed on the strip-retrieving finger(s) before beginning to fish. It is amazing how abrasive salt can be when rubbed on bare skin.

Without hesitation, I would name the pink as the easiest salmon species to hook while fly fishing. It is not the individuals, but the sheer numbers in a school that make it easy to hook a single fish. Pink salmon travel in schools, sometimes with as few as fifty members or as many as hundreds. A cast into a cruising school invariably results in a strike!

Coho travel in schools but their schools are much smaller, often having only a few individuals. They also travel as singles.

I have found that the fly reel is a major part of the fight. I always play all salmon from the reel. Beach fishing is shallow water fishing and for this I have found that the short five- or ten-foot sink tip fly lines are the most effective, or a weight forward dry line with a weighted fly also works well. Leader length is important in the clear saltwater and should be at least ten feet or more of at least #8 pound strength. My favorite beach fly continues to be the Pink Eve pattern. Recently I have found a red or pink glass bead optic pattern most effective, tied on a long-shank Mustad #34011 stainless steel # 4 or # 6 hook.

Without a doubt, Pacific salmon fly fishing is still in a pioneering state. The special lure of this fishery can best be described by the following open ocean experience my partner and I shared.

A Salmon of a Lifetime

A nor'west wind blew at about fifteen knots down the open waters of Sutil Channel. Tucking in the lee of a northern Gulf Island, we fly fished the low tide shallows, covering schools of young herring that had been driven to the intertidal zone by hungry, prodding salmon. These baitfish-herring schools, some covering an area as large as a house, were moving back and forth in the clear saltwater, swimming with the ebb and flow of the tidal current. Sometimes they were forced into depths no more than a meter and it was at these shallow schools that we targeted our casts.

I motored the boat to a position parallel with the bait schools and told my fly fishing partner, Bob Weir, to drop the anchor. By the time the anchor caught on our drift and the boat jolted to a halt in the wind, bow first, bobbing slightly with each large wave that crested the shallows, we were both casting toward the feeding melee. The constant darting of the coho was evident by sudden surface sprays of young herring leaping to escape.

Casting my Silver Thorn Flashtail fly into one surface bait spray, I felt the rod suddenly stop and I braced when the vibrations of a head-shaking coho telegraphed along the full length of the sink tip fly line and rod. Then it was off. But before I could gain control of the line, another took the fly and breached the water in a series of short leaps. The wind and flood tide waves continued to rock the boat, creating what I can only describe as a predator flash from the boat's white hull. It was obvious this spooked the concentrated baitfish, forcing the ever-harassed young herring to move further along the beach. As I reeled in my fly line, I called to Bob to pull up the anchor so we could motor once again to where the coho were now actively feeding, about 100 yards away. "Just one last cast," was Bob's comment as I prepared to start the motor.

The big tail of a chinook slapped the surface as Bob's fly bit hard! Bob had felt the take of the fish. Uncertain whether it was an intertidal beach rock at the first strike, he knew what it was when the salmon shook its head in apparent disbelief at this herring that bit back. The tail smash of the large chinook on the strike was incredible! It occurred in less than a yard of water and seemed to toss the school of young herring that were unfortunate enough to be in the way, in a vast crescent spray.

"Hurry, Barry, he's running!" This was Bob's exclamation, as I started the motor and quickly stepped up to the front to lift the anchor.

"He's into the backing!" Bob yelled, now in an obvious state of controlled panic!

I fought the rocking boat and pulled to loosen the cement block anchor. Then it was clear; I pulled the anchor up.

"Hurry, hurry!" Bob kept calling, "He hasn't even stopped his first run yet!"

The adrenalin cry of the reel quickened my pace and, after struggling to drive clear of one of the low tide boulders, I finally had the nose of the boat pointed toward the running chinook. Powering the boat, I was soon in a "spring chase" using the boat to follow this trophy salmon. This is a technique we use to force them to keep their head below the surface so that the fly will not slip out.

"Easy, easy!" was Bob's caution as I motored after the fish. "You made it just in time, I was down to my last fifty feet!"

What began then was a long and dramatic fight with a three-and-a-half-ounce fly rod and what proved to be a twenty-eight-pound chinook. It took forty minutes to finally bring that trophy to the net, after many spectacular unchinooklike leaps and numerous long runs. When it was over, we had drifted with the increasing wind to more than fifty-five yards in depth, from our original two yards, and we were at least a half a mile from the location where the fish had first taken the fly.

It was a summer salmon fly fishing experience that we will both remember for a long time! It proved once again, as did the twenty-three coho we also hooked fly fishing in these same waters during our two-day trip, that West Coast fly fishers have an untapped saltwater fly fishery waiting, just waiting....

Pacific Salmon Saltwater Fly Fishing Tackle

1) Rods: 9 to 10 ft.
   Pink salmon: ASA #6 or #7
   Coho, sockeye, chum salmon: ASA #8 or #9
   Chinook salmon: ASA #8, #9, or #10

2) Reels: Smooth, rust-free, capable of 300 yards or more of backing.

3) Fly lines: Matching ASA rod rating, or one ASA number up or down.
   a. Pink and coho beach fishing
      i) Weight forward floating and sink tips
   b. Open ocean feeders
      i) Weight forward floating and sink tips
      ii) Fast-sinking weight forward, sink rate #4, or higher
      iii) Shooting heads–350 grains, 500 grains, 700 grains
      iv) Protective finger-stripping guards

Above: Barry Thornton displays his salmon fly box. Note the preference for the Silver Thorn in its numerous variations.
Photo: Barry M. Thornton

Left: Silver bright June coho comes to hand in Tofino.
Photo: Harry Penner

Below: Hovering gulls and sea ducks are a sure sign of a concentration of baitfish . . . and, likely, salmon. *Photo: Barry M. Thornton*

Above: Leapers—the obvious sign of a school of salmon waiting.

Photo: Barry M. Thornton

Left: Mark Pendlington plays a June coho in Clayquot Sound. *Photo: Harry Penner*

Below: Herring ball being pushed to the surface by feeding coho salmon.

Photo: Barry M. Thornton

Above: No salmon here—indicated by the presence of a Pacific dogfish.

Photo: Barry M. Thornton

Right: Barry Thornton and Mark Pendlington bucktail and skipfly for coho in Tofino.

Photo: Harry Penner

Below: Barry Thornton's box of weighted and unweighted salmon flies.

Photo: Barry M. Thornton

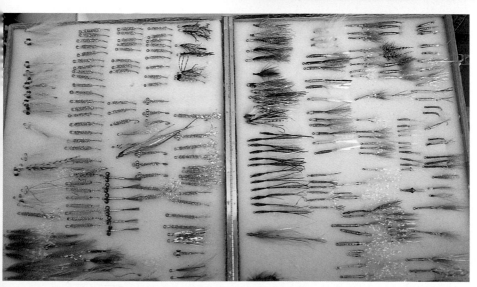

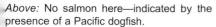

99

Above: Coastal estuaries like this one at the Oyster River draw thousands of salmon and hundreds of beach salmon fly fishers every year. *Photo: Barry M. Thornton*

Left: Lise Peters of Moonlight Flies holds a chrome bright pink salmon. Note the cobblestone beach common in many estuary/beach fly fishing areas along the West Coast. *Photo: Moonlight Flies*

Below: Deceiver patterns tied by Lise Peters. *Photo: Moonlight Flies*

100

Kelly Davison anchored and casting to coho in open saltwater.

Photo: Harry Penner

Silver bright Tofino coho nears the boat.

Photo: Barry M. Thornton

Above: Weigh West Resorts in Tofino with their specially designed fly fishing boats.

Photo: Harry Penner

Left: Coho salmon taken on one of Barry Thornton's Pink Eve patterns.

Photo: Moonlight Flies

Below: Kelp beds hold bait fish and are a prime target run for coho salmon.

Photo: Harry Penner

Fully anodized saltwater reel, a must for the avid saltwater fly fisher. *Photo: Harry Penner*

Above: Sunset on the West Coast can be a dramatic sight! *Photo: Moonlight Flies*

Left: Epoxy fry, euphasids and krill patterns tied by Shawn Bennett of Moonlight Flies. *Photo: Moonlight Flies*

West Coast Rivers for Salmon

by Harry Penner

There are virtually thousands of rivers up and down the West Coast—all of which are inhabited by Pacific salmon. These rivers not only deserve your attention as an angler, but also deserve your respect. I am hopeful that the information in the following pages will help improve your odds of catching fish, as well as give you some insight into what a wonderful sport-fish Pacific salmon are.

I fish two different methods for salmon: cast and retrieve, or cast and swing. I also keep my fly patterns to a minimum. As a guide, it is important to make it as easy as possible for clients to catch fish. Getting too technical simply confuses most people and makes for a long day.

Lines

This is where most of the confusion starts, primarily because there are as many opinions on fly lines as there are lines. Every manufacturer makes a variety of lines, from floating to full sinking, as well as a number of sink tip lines. Each of the latter is available in different rates of sinking density.

In an effort to simplify, I will not try to explain all the different types and combinations of lines on the market. Instead, I'm going to elaborate on the system that I have found works best for me. This is not to say you should not experiment for yourself (that's half the fun), but you should have a solid base from which to start and expand your own understanding of fly fishing for salmon.

Fly fishing lines are probably open to the most personal experimentation. For the sake of argument, I am going to explain the system in which I have become confident. However, in time you can develop a system that will work best for you. I will also touch a little on making your own sink tip lines for a fraction of the cost of tailor-made ones.

Following are some items that are an integral part of my arsenal. (1) Scientific Anglers Mastery series WF-9-F Steelhead Taper floating line is the best long-distance casting line I have used. (2) Scientific Anglers WF-9-S Monocore, a monofilament fly line for fishing clear stillwaters or beach fishing, is also a favorite. (3) Teeny Nymph Company WF-9-F/S Mini Tip is a five-foot sink tip that works well for fishing subsurface. (4) Scientific Anglers WF-8-F/S Wet Tip type 4 13-foot, when cut down to 9-foot, fills the gap between the mini tip and my heavier lines. (5) Teeny Nymph Company T-200, T-300, T-400 & T-500 make up the remainder. All of these lines are twenty-four-foot sink tips, ranging from 200 to 500 grains. Of all the sink tip lines I have tried, these lines made by Jim Teeny are the easiest to cast and also make it possible to fish all types of water when getting down to the fish is paramount. With the lines mentioned above, I can deal with any water, whether skating a dry fly or greased liner or dredging bottom in all but the fastest water that can still be considered fishable.

As for making your own lines, all you need is a level floating running line. Scientific Anglers makes a nice thirty-foot, 750-grain shooting head. First, cut the shooting head into three pieces, five-foot, ten-foot and fifteen-foot sections. Attach braided nylon loops to the ends of each piece as well as the level running line on your reel. This way you can loop the different tips to your floating line and in effect make your own sink tip lines of different densities. While it isn't always the easiest thing to cast, it does give you numerous options at very little cost. However, you will still need a floating line, for level running lines don't cast very well as they do not have tapered shooting heads. Another option for a line is to take a floating line, cut off the tapered head and attach loops to the two pieces where you made the cut. You now have a floating head as well as the sink tips. Not only will this save you a small fortune on fly lines but you only need one reel body and one spool.

Leaders

I used to spend much time with leaders. I guess I thought all fish were leader shy. Well many years and a small fortune spent on commercial tapered leaders later, I have come to the conclusion that it just does not matter. Fish don't care what kind of leader you use. The same can be said for tippet material. Save your money and just buy a few spools of monofilament and tie your own leaders. It is really quite easy.

I use two different leader systems. One system is for sink tip lines and one is for my dry and monocore line. Regardless of which line I am fishing, all my fly lines have a three-foot butt section of 20-lb. monocore. When fishing a sink tip, your leader need not be too long, that is, rarely more than six feet. So all you have to do is tie in to the butt section two to four feet of whatever test monofilament you feel is necessary. When I am using my monocore line, as I do when I cast and retrieve, I prefer a longer leader. To achieve this I tie in about four feet of 15-lb. test to the butt section and then another four feet of 6-lb. test. This gives me a leader of about eleven feet in all. It will nicely turn over any fly measuring up to size #4. I tend to tie my butt section to the fly line with a nail knot and the rest are all blood knots–unless I am feeling lazy. Then, I have been known to use a double surgeon's knot.

Rods

I remember my first fly rod, a fiberglass model of questionable quality, purchased at the Army and Navy store, and a Daiwa 732 reel. (I blew the rod into a million pieces on a chum salmon.) These days I use two rods exclusively for all my river salmon fly fishing: a Loomis GLX 10-ft. #8 and 10-ft. #9. I know for some of the smaller species of salmon this may seem like a bit of overkill, but I'm matching the rod to the line more often than I am to the fish. For example, I spend a fair bit of time fishing the Fraser River for sockeye in August. The fish, for the most part, are not much more than three kilograms, so a nine weight isn't really necessary to land the fish, is it? The reason I use the larger rod is to facilitate the use of a high-density sink tip line. Because the fish are sitting in deep, fast-running water, I need a heavy line to get to them. This would not be possible with a #6 or #7 rod.

The way I break down my system of rods to lines is as follows: all my heavy sink tip lines are used with my #9 rod. One thing I have discovered is that not all heavy weight rods are up to the task of casting some of the heavier sink tip lines. I have had the opportunity to use many different top-quality rods, and in a lot of cases I have come away disappointed. As many fly fishers can attest, casting any high density line is a test of a person's character. No finesse here, just chuck and duck.

My dry line, light sink tips and an intermediate-full sink tips are put to use on my #8 rod. I only dropped down one line weight for a few different reasons. (1) If I break a rod, I still want to be able to utilize all of the lines in my arsenal. If I carried a #7 for a second rod, some of my lines would probably overload the rod and therefore be useless. (2) Because I fish a lot of big water, long casts can be very advantageous and the ten-foot #8 rod is the best rod when making long casts. (3) After salmon fishing, my next love is steelhead, and it is a great line weight for summer-run steelhead.

The above paragraphs will give you some insight into what you need to take into consideration when it comes to purchasing a rod for yourself. One thing I cannot stress enough is to make sure the rod you purchase has an anodized reel seat (i.e., has a protective finish), a cork handle and stainless steel snake guides. I can appreciate that not everyone can afford the luxury of some of the more expensive rods the market has to offer. It takes a lot of guiding for me to justify having the rods for myself and my clients. At the end of the day if you can manage it, I strongly recommend making the investment in a top quality rod—you will never regret it.

Reels

Contrary to popular belief, a salmon reel is not just a place to store fly line. A trout reel maybe, but not a reel you have aspirations of landing big fish on. But this doesn't mean you must spend a ridiculous amount of money. There are plenty of reasonably priced models available.

Following are a few things to keep in mind when you make a purchase. (1) Will you be using this reel in saltwater? If so, consider buying a reel that is fully anodized. Nothing will destroy a reel faster than saltwater. I have had plenty of personal experience in bringing some of my prized reels to a premature end by using them beach fishing. It doesn't seem to matter how much I rinse them, I still end up with damage. (2) Make sure the reel has enough capacity to hold at least 100 meters of backing under your fly line. Most manufacturers will include a table in the packaging that shows how much 20-lb. backing will fit onto the reel in relation to a number of different weights of fly lines. For example, the reel will hold 150 meters of backing with a #7 floating line but only 100 meters with a #8 floating line and even less with a #9. All sinking and sink tip lines have a smaller diameter than floating lines, so if your dry line fits onto the spool and allows enough backing you will have no problems with your other lines. (3) As you will have more than one fly line, you will need more than one spool for your reel. Some people still strip the line off the reel and wind on another one when needed. There's nothing wrong with this, but at times it is not very practical, and with the advent of reels that use plastic cassette spools, cost is no longer a factor. Cassettes rarely cost more than ten dollars. However, if you're not fond of this system, be sure that the reel you buy has extra spools available. (4) Drag systems— all reels are not created equally in this capacity. Generally there are two types of drag systems. A disc drag incorporates a cork or synthetic disc that acts as a brake pad between the spool and the reel body. A clicker drag uses a metal pall to exert pressure against a gear on the back side of the spool. For the most part, all this type of drag does is guard against back lashes and does not afford the angler any kind of controllable drag.

As with the rods, always buy the best you can afford; however, this is an area where you can make do with less. The reel is an integral part of your equipment, but it isn't as vital to the actual hooking of the fish as are the rod, line and flies.

Flies

A person could write volumes on flies (in fact people have). Fly preferences are as varied as the individuals that tie them. Personally, I feel that tying different flies and field testing them can sometimes be the most rewarding aspect of fly fishing. To make something with your own hands, from your own imagination, and then catch a fish on it is always a thrill no matter how long you have been doing it. Even the shortcomings are part of the learning curve and should not be looked upon as failures.

I have always fished with very few patterns, and learned to fish them to the best of my ability. I find if there are too many flies in the fly box, I get a headache from all the self-doubt. Am I using the right fly, maybe I should change to the green one? No, the yellow. How about red? You see where I'm going? Don't go there, it will drive you nuts. Become confident in a few patterns and learn how to fish them effectively for each species of salmon under a variety of water conditions.

Generally, when I am fishing fast water with a heavy line, I believe it's more important to get the fly down to the fish and use the right color than to have the proper pattern. The fly is swinging quite quickly and the fish do not have much time to react, therefore I usually use leech patterns, consisting mainly of marabou. This gives the fly a lot of movement. It comes in every color imaginable and is easy for anyone to tie. Another consideration when choosing a fly is the condition in which the fly will be used. When fishing fast waters with heavy lines, you will inevitably lose a lot of flies, and you don't want them to be something you slaved over for hours.

Fishing still or slack water is another story altogether. This is a situation where you will be forced to cast and retrieve. That is to say you cast to a group of fish and pull the fly away from them hoping to entice one to follow. This gives the fish plenty of opportunity to inspect and (more often than not) refuse your offering. It is under these circumstances that fly patterns are of paramount concern, and in my experience the sparser the pattern the better. I prefer minnow or small streamer flies.

Coho Salmon

Coho are the most sought-after of all the salmonoids in fresh water. They are known for long, searing runs and acrobatic maneuvers that leave even the most seasoned angler shaken before they are finally brought to the net. To me, coho are what fly fishing for salmon is all about.

Like their larger cousin the chinook, coho fry will live for at least a year in freshwater, usually in a small stream. In some cases coho will inhabit the estuary of a stream or move into an adjacent lake. This is often because of poor water conditions in the stream, i.e., warm water or even drying up of water in summer months.

Unlike sockeye, coho do not have enormous localized runs like that of the Adams or Babine rivers. Coho inhabit almost any small stream, river or creek that drains into the Fraser, Skeena and many smaller river basins. Urbanization, unethical forest practices and ever-increasing agricultural demands have had some devastating effects on the runs. Decimation of our coho stocks have taken place over a long period of time without any alarm bells going off, as they have with sockeye when a large run fails to materialize. It would truly be a crime to lose this species of Pacific salmon.

With very few exceptions, I do all my coho fishing in still or slack water. When coho are at rest or just generally mulling around, they are the most susceptible to a cast and retrieved fly. Now this doesn't mean you only fish pools. Fish the slack water on the inside bend in a river. I've found coho stacked up in a foot of water first thing in the morning, before anyone has spooked them. Fish the side channels and any pocket off the main channel, such as a piece of slack water created by a log jam or some other obstruction. Anywhere the current noticeably slows down affords the fish a place to rest. Cut banks caused by erosion offer excellent cover for coho. If found adjacent to a slack water pool, these areas can be very productive by simply casting against the bank and pulling the fly away. This is not to say that a coho won't slip behind a rock in the main channel like other salmonoids and rest—they will. However, trying to present the fly to them properly under these conditions is almost impossible.

The sloughs of the Fraser Valley are a wonderful place to pursue coho. The current is slow and allows perfect conditions for a cast and retrieve fly. Before I forget, I would like to address one mistake that I see made over and over again. You have just spent half the morning hiking into a favorite coho hole, the water looks like glass, you can even see the occasional fish porpoise, everything is perfect. Don't, I repeat, don't walk in waist-deep and start casting. Always fish your way in. Some mornings all the fish will be close to shore in very little water. Not only will you be missing an opportunity to catch more fish, but you run the risk of putting the fish down for the day. Not a pleasant thought when I think of the trouble I've gone to bushwacking my way into some of my favorite haunts.

When fishing slack water, the fish have the opportunity to inspect everything I have to offer, therefore I get concerned about the spooking factor. To minimize this, I use a monocore fly line (monofilament fly line) and a nine- to twelve-foot leader. I also use very subtle fly patterns, such as Muddler Minnows, Mickey Fins, small epoxy minnows and on occasion a Woolly Bugger. But probably the single most important element is the retrieve. Most people get into a rut and don't vary their retrieve. Keep mixing it up. Strip fast. If that doesn't work, slow it down. I usually strip quite fast, about eight inches at a time, and retrieve it right to the nail knot on your fly line. I don't let the line sink too far before I start stripping my fly back in. I don't want the fish to see my fly stationary and figure out it is a dud. Sometimes retrieving your fly from a different angle will help when fish aren't cooperating. I honestly believe that if you know the fish are out there, you can catch a large majority of them by just sticking with it and making minor changes in your tactics.

Chinook Salmon

These fish are more commonly referred to as king or spring salmon, and when they exceed thirty pounds they are called tyee, a Native word meaning chief. The chinook's spawning grounds range from the Sacramento River in California to the Yukon River in Alaska. Although chinook salmon inhabit almost 1,000 rivers and streams in North America, the largest and most important runs are in the Sacramento, Columbia, Fraser, Skeena, Nushagvat and Yukon rivers. The greatest chinook river of all time was the Columbia. All through the late 1800s commercial fishing intensified, and while the stocks did drop, the overall population of chinook remained strong. That is until the advent of hydroelectric dams. These blocked access to thousands of miles of salmon habitat and brought an end to the greatest run of chinook salmon on the West Coast. Fortunately, the mighty Fraser and Skeena rivers were spared the devastation of the Columbia. However, they have not escaped unscathed. Habitat degradation from questionable logging practices, increasing pressure from both commercial and Native fisheries, as well as a portion of sport fishermen that haven't come to terms with a catch-and-release fishery, have all taken their toll.

In most cases, chinook salmon spawn in the fall and early winter months. Upon hatching, the young salmon remain in their gravel nursery for up to three months or until they have absorbed their yolk sac. At this point, the juvenile salmon work their way up through the gravel to the free-flowing stream and begin the journey to the ocean. Some fry proceed straight to the sea while others will remain in the river more than a year before beginning the downstream migration. Once in the open ocean, the juveniles feed on small fish and crustaceans, all the while being predated on themselves by various fish and diving marine birds. Adult chinook feed on invertebrates like shrimp and squid, but their primary source of food is the Pacific herring.

After three to five years of voracious feeding at sea, the adult chinook return to the river of their birth. For some, this can mean a journey of several thousand miles, past a gauntlet of seemingly insurmountable hurdles. Once back on the spawning beds, the males and females pair off and the task of laying and fertilizing eggs begins. The females die within a week or two of spawning, but the males can often live for weeks before completing their cycle.

Of the five species of Pacific salmon, the chinook is without a doubt the most difficult to catch on the fly. Not only because of their apparent disinterest in most fly patterns, but also because they prefer to hold in the deepest runs. This means concentrating your efforts fishing the head to middle of the run. Don't waste time in the tail-outs; these fish like deep water. When fishing smaller rivers like the Vedder-Chilliwack and Chehalis in the Fraser Valley, it is relatively easy to determine where to start fishing. The entire river system is a series of runs and rapids that flow into the head of a run, thus carving out a nice, deep trough for the chinook to lie in. As the water loses its pace, it widens out, becomes shallower and forms a tail-out.

Fishing "big or bigger water" presents fly fishers with many challenges. Rivers like the Thompson or Harrison don't offer the angler any easily recognizable runs—it all tends to look alike. Even the Stamp-Somas River on Vancouver Island can be a little perplexing if you don't know what to look for. I often talk about fishing the inside bend of a river and I've been reminded, more than once, that I have to be more specific about what I mean by that. When the river makes a turn, no matter how sharp or slight, the water on the outside of the turn has to travel faster than the water on the inside. What this does is cause a slick or patch of slower moving water to form on the inside bend, and very often it will have a glassy appearance. Where the slack water meets the faster water is called a seam, and that is where you will find not only chinook, but other species of salmon (not to mention steelhead). It allows them a place to rest out of the main flow but within easy access of the main channel to continue their upstream migration.

So much time fly fishing is spent looking for fish, you don't want to be wasting your day just improving your casting. With a little bit of practice and using your own common sense, it doesn't take long before you can eliminate certain stretches of water by just looking at them, thus saving yourself valuable fishing time.

Fly fishing for chinook salmon is similar to fishing for winter-run steelhead. You have to get the fly down to the fish. Therefore it is important to choose a line that will get you to within a foot of the river bottom. Remember, if your line does not get hung up once in a while, you are not doing it right. I like to cast slightly up the stream and quickly throw a couple of upstream mends into the line. This allows the line to sink quickly and get down to the fish. If the line picks up speed in the current and you feel it bump bottom just as it starts to swing, you are in the zone. Sometimes I retrieve the line a little as it swings to impart some added action on the fly and hopefully attract some fish's attention. When the fly swings down below me, I pick up the line, take a few steps down stream and cast again. This isn't rocket science, just a very effective and time proven way of fishing a fly on the swing. My fly of choice is a Popsicle or any other large leech pattern.

Sockeye Salmon

When the average person thinks of salmon, they think of millions of crimson red salmon descending on the coastal rivers of British Columbia and Alaska. Some runs travel tens of thousands of miles by the time they complete their journey from the high seas to the rivers of their origin. Is it any wonder no other salmon on earth has been the subject of as much literature (or for that matter folklore) than the remarkable sockeye?

Sockeye salmon, as a rule, spawn in rivers that either feed or are fed by a large lake. Shortly after emerging from the gravel the fry will migrate to the lake and use it as their own personal nursery for the next year. This can trigger some incredible trout fishing, as trout lay in wait for the fry at creek mouths emptying into the lake.

The sockeye is one of the few salmon species that seems to be making a recovery, in some instances its numbers are back to historical levels. This is due in part to man's intervention with the building of fish ladders around obstacles that were the cause of high mortality. As well, hatchery programs have helped to augment existing stocks. The revitalization of habitat previously lost to poor logging practices has also had an enormous impact on the rebound of certain runs of the sockeye salmon—the Adams, Babine and Horse Fly in particular. The one downside is the incidental catch of weaker runs of coho, chinook and steelhead in the commercial bonanza that plies for the prized sockeye at the mouth of both the Fraser and Skeena rivers. I am hopeful that the boom for the sockeye doesn't mean bust for the rest of the sport fishery.

Mid- to late August is when you will find me searching the Fraser River in British Columbia on the lookout for cruising sockeye salmon. The gravel bars around Chilliwack in the Fraser Valley are always a good place to start a sockeye search. Because the annual freshet changes the river from year to year, productive runs from previous years may not hold any fish this year. Therefore, preseason scouting can really pay dividends.

The sockeye sport fishery has a very strong following, and finding a good place to fish is as simple as finding other anglers. One trip upriver and you'll know which spots are productive by the number of anglers on some of the gravel bars. If you are trying to get away from the masses and want to strike out on your own, here are some things to keep in mind. Gravel bars with a moderate pace of water flow, a depth of four to six feet and a bottom of softball-sized rocks are preferred resting and travel lanes. Very seldom do I find any number of fish holding on sandy bottoms or slack water.

The most important element of fly fishing sockeye is getting the fly down to where they travel (about a foot off the bottom) and keeping it there as long as possible. This means using the cast and swing method, and a sink tip line that will get down to the fish quickly and stay down as it swings. My fly of choice is any leech or streamer pattern in a chartreuse for dirty water and a Popsicle in clear conditions. Some will argue that a large number of sockeye are being flossed and are not aggressively taking the fly. On those days when the Fraser is running a little high and visibility is virtually zero, I would have to agree. But then there are the days when the fish are only taking a certain color of fly. I have found, however, that some strains of sockeye take better than others. The Horse Fly run is the most aggressive that I have fished for, and the Harrison-Weaver salmon runs are the toughest to catch.

Another impediment to catching sockeye to take into consideration is the commercial fishery on the lower Fraser. After an opening, fishing can come to an absolute stop for two or three days. It can be very frustrating when this happens on the only days you have off. Keep in mind that sockeye come through in waves, and as a result some days are substantially better than others.

Sockeye aren't the largest of the Pacific salmon, averaging around five pounds. When hooked, however, not many fish can compare to the fight and aerial show put on by the sockeye, and that includes steelhead.

Chum Salmon

This salmon is probably the most widely distributed and definitely the most maligned of all the Pacific salmon. Their common name, dog salmon, comes from the word *keta*, which is Russian for dog, and their rather ragged appearance as they reach the peak of their spawning cycle. Their most notable attributes are a set of fierce-looking teeth and vivid purple bars along their sides. Although chum salmon inhabit a wide range of rivers on the West Coast of North America, with very few exceptions, they do not travel great distances upstream to spawn, preferring the lower reaches of coastal rivers and in some instances even tidal water. Dog salmon are also one of the larger species of salmon, averaging eleven pounds, and surprisingly, up until a few years ago they were not avidly pursued by anglers, myself included.

Until I started guiding, I never really considered the chum much of a sport fish. That is until much of my clientele decided they would rather catch chum than some of the other smaller salmon that were readily available. I guess it is a "big fish" thing. Until I figured out how to catch them on a fairly regular basis and not foul-hook so many, fishing for them was pretty much lost on me.

The best thing about fishing for chum salmon is that one can catch them in both still and fast water. Utilizing the cast and swing method, as described for chinook, you can be very successful fishing all but the fastest runs. You will find that the fish you hook in deeper, faster water are for the most part cleaner and more energetic fish.

Whether in the lower reaches of the Chilliwack-Vedder system or fishing the back waters of the Stave River, I love hooking big fish in still water. More often the by-product of fishing for coho in still water, I found that if I used larger flies with lots of movement (i.e., leeches, Woolly Buggers, etc.) I could catch chum salmon almost at will and with very few foul-hooked fish. The trick is to vary your retrieve. One day they want it fast, the next day slow. Working a bead head or weighted leech through a pool on a dry line with an undulating motion, much like you would work a leech on an interior lake, can have spectacular results.

Chum fishing is getting more popular every year. The size of the fish and its searing runs make it easy to understand why.

Pink Salmon

Called pinks or humpies, for the large hump that males develop just prior to spawning, these salmon are the smallest (about three to five pounds) and most prolific of the Pacific salmon. Unlike the other species of salmon which mature after four or five years at sea, the pink function on a two-year life cycle and return to their river after only a couple of years of ocean feeding. Pink salmon return to the Fraser and other south coast rivers by the millions every odd-numbered year and to the northern and Vancouver Island rivers on even-numbered years. Because of their two-year cycle, during off years these same rivers have few or no fish returning.

Pink salmon are plankton feeders, and for that reason their flesh is pale in comparison with other salmon, which makes them the least desirable to the commercial fleet.

Spawning takes place from August through November. Females prepare several nests and spawn with more than one male. The adults die shortly after spawning.

Almost immediately after emerging from the gravel, pink fry start their journey to coastal waters. They travel mostly at night, but will migrate during the daylight hours if they have a long distance to travel. Feeding takes place sporadically if at all, and then usually on aquatic insects. In turn, the young salmon become forage for other residents, as well as migratory fish in the river system.

The lower Fraser River offers some of the best pink fishing along the coast. Almost any gravel bar with a moderate to slack water flow will have thousands of pink salmon within reach of the fly fisherman. Because humpies inhabit the entire water column, getting the fly down to the bottom of the river is of little importance. A dry line or light sink tip is all that is needed. Cast slightly downstream, mend your line a couple of times so that your fly line is swinging straight, and make a slow retrieve. This is more to keep in contact with the fly than to give the fly any action. The take can be quite light.

Pink are very easy to catch and are a great introduction to fly fishing for children or novices. The fly I prefer is an Epoxy Minnow with a bushy pink marabou tail. Almost any pink color fly will work, but I find I go through less flies when the fly has an epoxy body.

Keep It Simple

Fly fishing can be as simple or as complicated as you make it. As you have probably figured out by reading this, I try to keep things simple because as a guide, I have to make it as easy as possible for clients to catch fish. The easier the method, the more quickly people catch on, the more fish they catch and the more fun they have. At the end of the day, that is what it is really all about—enjoying the outdoors with friends and exchanging lies about the one that got away.

PRIME-TIME CHART
(South Coast Region)

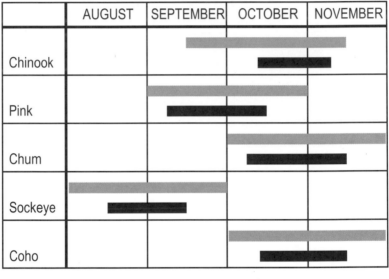

	AUGUST	SEPTEMBER	OCTOBER	NOVEMBER
Chinook				
Pink				
Chum				
Sockeye				
Coho				

Season ▬▬▬▬   Prime-time ▬▬▬▬

The silver bright reward of fly fishing for coho on West Coast rivers. *Photo: Harry Penner*

Group of anglers enjoying a day's pink salmon fly fishing on the gravel bars of the Fraser River near Chilliwack.
Photo: Harry Penner

Playing a sockeye salmon on the Fraser River. Note how shallow these gravel bars are when presenting the fly.   *Photo: Harry Penner*

Harry Penner's friend Jim Teeny with a 35-pound chinook.
Photo: Harry Penner

Jet sleds like these are ideal for navigating B.C.'s shallow coastal rivers.
Photo: Harry Penner

Opposite top: A classic salmon run on the upper Pitt River.

Opposite bottom: Mark Pendlington with a beautiful coho taken in the backwaters of the Fraser Valley.

Right: A bonus Dolly Varden often caught while fly fishing for salmon on south coast rivers.

Below inset: Silver bright coho salmon taken in late November in the sloughs in the Fraser Valley.

Bottom: Don Norwood plays a chrome coho on the inside bend of a river. Note the slick glassy appearance where the fast water meets the slow.

Following page: Harry Penner fly fishing a crystal clear run on a pristine B.C. stream.

Photos: Harry Penner

Mt. Cheam, a Fraser Valley landmark for those fly fishing Simon Fraser's river for Pacific salmon.
Photo: Harry Penner

The Sea-run Cutthroat Trout

by Kelly Davison

The underdog of the anadromous salmonid world, the sea-run cutthroat trout (*Oncorhynchus clarki clarki*) has always fascinated many Northwest anglers. Ranging from Alaska to California, this sporty West Coast trout flourishes along the bays and inlets that indent the coastline. Hatched in the smallest of urban streams to the largest of coastal rivers, the sea-run struggles for its existence. As soon as it emerges, the cutthroat is pushed out of the prime rearing areas by the more aggressive coho juveniles. The cutthroat is then forced to rear in less-comfortable river environs. With little food, less water and less cover, the cutts are subject to predation from many of the stream's inhabitants.

Not all cutthroat are of the sea-run variety. Some cutthroat remain in the headwaters of streams, thus growing very little and reaching a maximum length of about ten inches. These small, dark trout are heavily spotted and have vivid red slashes under the lower jaw. Having no access to the bounty of the sea, these cutts live out their lives being the predator in their miniature environment. Cutthroat that inhabit coastal lakes can attain much larger sizes due to the quantity and quality of food in the still waters. Some of the lakes have natural barriers on their outlet streams that effectively block any passage to or from the sea. A few lakes in B.C.'s Powell River area have cutthroat in the ten- to twelve-pound range. Feeding on sticklebacks and coarse fish, these trout grow rapidly and offer the angler some wonderful sport.

In its saltwater environment, the sea-run cutthroat inhabits areas strewn with small stones and prefers gently sloping beaches with few large rocks. This occurs, perhaps, because large rocks often harbor predators, such as bullheads and rock fish. Sea-runs occupy a niche like no other adult salmonid, favoring shallow clear water with sunken structures and weathered toredo-bored rocks. One such area is on the Sechelt Peninsula, where I have witnessed the cutthroat taking up feeding stations behind such structures as the flooding autumn-tide-brought dinner to the waiting trout. Largely opportunistic feeders, the sea-run's diet consists of sculpins, crab megalops, sticklebacks, Euphasid shrimp and sand lance.

For the angler, the beach cutthroat is one of the most exciting fish to pursue. There is something about a crisp fall morning, when the leaves have turned and the mountains are reflected on the flat, calm surface of the sea. Walking down the steep trail, you try to catch a glimpse of the beach through the salmonberry bushes. On the beach, small patches of mist are rising off the mirrored water. It is morning and the tide is flooding. Suddenly, you see a swirl off to the left within casting range. You watch and wait to make sure it wasn't one of the grebes that make this place their home. No bird—so you make the cast.

The floating line falls gently on the water. When you start your foot-long retrieve, the leader straightens with the fly making a small V on the surface. Suddenly another V appears behind the fly! Then a nose! Picking up the pace and increasing the speed of your retrieve, you feel the nail-knot connection of your leader hit the tip of your fly rod and you realize you have run out of fly line. The fly stops, then the fish turns and swirls, disappearing in the mist.

If you haven't completely lost your composure, which most of us do, you fire a cast in the direction of the fleeing fish. The fly lands with a plop and he is on it. Taking it instantly and solidly, the cutt is out of the water and on his tail; the still air broken by the leaping sea-run. The fish tires quickly after a few short runs and you bring him quietly to hand. Cradling him gently, you admire the heavy dark spotting that runs right to his belly. A yellow hue over the dark spots blends distinctively with his yellow-tinged fins. Behind the dorsal fin, high up above the lateral line, a dime-size disclike parasite is attached to the skin. You turn him over and see under the lower jaw the faint pinkish orange slashes that distinguish him as a cutthroat. Gently removing the barbless hook you admire this sea-run wonder as it swims away.

The sea-run cutthroat is not a large fish, most average thirteen to eighteen inches. A number of fish in the five-pound range still exist but are few and far between. In the wild, a cutthroat can take two years to reach about a foot in length. Some cutthroat may live seven or eight years and make frequent journeys from saltwater to fresh. Repeat spawning is common, and a mature female may spawn four times in her lifetime. The male cutthroat is less likely to spawn as often as the female because the spawning males tend to stay in the stream longer. Because of their lengthy stay, the males are then subject to lower stream flows and higher mortality.

Most saltwater salmonid grow quickly after reaching the food-rich ocean environment. The sea-run cutthroat does not because, unlike the Pacific salmon, the cutthroat will move back into its home stream for many months where there is less food and little opportunity for growth. Sea-runs have the unique physiological ability to move from saltwater to freshwater and back to saltwater with ease. Cutthroat seem to prefer moving along areas of brackish water and close to shore, and avoid the deeper ocean crossings. Traveling schools of trout will frequent an area for a time, feeding on the available food such as migrating sculpin or out-migrant salmon fry. Very few cutthroat will winter in the ocean. By late fall, most will have moved into streams and rivers (but not necessarily their home streams) to feast on salmon eggs washed out of the salmon redds by the early winter rains.

Winter Trout

It was early January and there was a cold northerly outflow wind blowing. I made my way up the Harrison River to the mouth of the Chehalis River. The highway bridge howled eerily as gusts of wind hit the bridge rail and funneled down to Harrison Bay. The boat was being pounded with the water spray being blown off the tops of the waves. Reaching the relative shelter of Vincent's Spit, I eased my boat through the opening that led to the mouth of the Chehalis. A myriad of eagles was eating the last remnants of the late fall salmon run.

Recent heavy rains had caused the Chehalis River to become very high. After two days of clear, cold weather, I knew that the river level would drop and I hoped the cutthroat would be keying in on the thousands of salmon eggs dislodged from recently covered redds. After beaching the boat, I crossed a side channel and waded to the grassy cut bank that marked the deepest part of the channel. Peering down through the crystal clear water, I could see the occasional flash as the cutthroat rolled up off the bottom to pick up the free-drifting eggs.

My fly line of choice this day was a five-foot sink tip line. I tied on a short piece of 5X tippet, making the total leader length about three feet. A small, pale pink glow-bug fly was attached to the tippet. Casting upstream, the fly line immediately formed a belly, sweeping the fly up off the bottom of the river. (When a belly forms in a line, the fly line has become crescent-shaped as it floats on a stream's surface due to differences in currents within a stream.) With an upstream mend, I corrected the belly and the fly began to reach the same water level as the feeding fish. I saw a fish roll as he took the imitation. The belly of the floating portion of the fly line had hesitated slightly as he picked up the egg. Twisting and rolling in the heavy current, the smallish fish struggled, and as I slid him to the edge of the grass, his brilliant sides were shining silver. His back was blue-green fresh from the sea. His tiny button head looked out of proportion to his fat belly, gorged on salmon eggs—a beauty!

Fraser Cutthroat

The Fraser River, undammed in its main stem, offers unequaled winter cutthroat fishing. As the Lower Mainland fly angler waits patiently for ice-off to occur on the interior lakes, he or she can explore the Fraser. Chironomid fishing in February! Some of the back waters have amazing hatches of small midges at this time of year. Small stone flies and leeches also work well while fishing in the side channels and riffles. The Fraser is truly a wonder in winter, completely different from the silt-laden powerhouse of May to November. In the winter, the Fraser is at its lowest. Many of the gravel bars are exposed, causing riffles to form with very slowly moving water—ideal places to find cutthroat. Some of the back waters may be 100 yards from the main river, but as long as these back waters have good inflows or outflows of water they will be likely areas to find cutthroat.

With visibility sometimes as much as six feet, the winter Fraser is a joy to fish—rarely is the river this clean. The river can get dirty after heavy local rains, but as long as the interior of the province stays locked up in ice, the river's discoloration will disappear after a few days of sun. During cold snaps, which can last for a few weeks, the shore edges will freeze. Chunks of ice can break off and drift in the current. It is best to stay off the river at this time as it can be extremely dangerous, especially to boaters. Large ice floes are sucked down in the swirling eddies and shot up like missiles. When the above-freezing local temperatures return, the river clears of ice and the adventurous angler can search for the elusive cutthroat.

Sea-runs move. You can find them in one area one day and return the next day to find them gone. I once fished a large school for two weeks in a back channel near the Agassiz-Rosedale bridge in B.C.'s Upper Fraser Valley, but in the remaining month of the season, I could not find a single fish. From Hope to Strawberry Island, the cutthroat move about searching for food in the back waters, sloughs and main river. Effective flies, should include chironomids, small dark leeches, black stone flies and minnow imitations.

133

Remember, exploring is the key, observing is the lock that when unlatched, opens the door to this excellent fishery.

Tackle and Techniques

The cutthroat fly fisherman should outfit him or herself with all the necessary tackle required for chasing these seasonal trout. A light nine or nine and a half foot graphite rod with a line size of #4, #5 or #6 is ideal. I prefer the nine and a half foot #5 weight rod, as this longer rod allows the angler maximum control in moving water (where line mending is necessary to control the drift). Long rods allow better casting distance, which is an important factor while cutthroat fishing, especially in still water. The further the cast, the more time the cutt has to chase down and eat your fly. This weight rod will enable the smaller trout to "show their stuff" but it will still maintain enough backbone to subdue the larger trout.

The reel, which is the least important part of the whole outfit, should be corrosion resistant and, preferably, anodized. Other fly reel options include inexpensive exposed-rim reels— the reel is mainly for fly line storage. A spring and pawl drag system is suitable for most cutthroat trout angling. Some of the new reels on the market offer disc drag tension control, which gives the reel a smoother feel and allows for a wider range of drag settings. The disc drag system fly reel is also a good choice, especially for the saltwater angler, because that tiny rise you cast to could turn out to be a hooked nose coho.

The fly line is as important as the rod. A floating or dry line is the number one choice for all cutthroat fishing. A good quality fly line is a must as these lines will float higher, last longer and cast better than the inexpensive lines. Most importantly, the fly line should match the designated line size on the fly rod or one fly line size higher. For example, most better quality fly rods in a #5 weight will handle a #6 line. When using one line size higher, most anglers will feel the fly rod "load up" faster when a shorter length of fly line is extended outside of the rod tip. The difficulty may come when the angler is trying to hold a long length of fly line in the air, which may cause the rod to soften its action.

The "single haul" or "double haul" are casting techniques that will allow the angler to effectively increase line speed and shoot line to minimize false casting. Much less effort is required and with minimal false casting, the fly will be in the water longer and should therefore result in fewer fishless days.

The dry fly line does not limit the angler to floating flies only. Many cutthroat wet fly patterns can be fished effectively with floating lines and long leaders. Small weighted nymphs and minnow patterns are especially good flies when fished "dead drift," (the action of an artificial fly as it drifts unattended in the manner of a dead insect, without being affected by the fly line) in moving water, with the dry line. Also, controlling the drift of the line and fly is made much easier with the floating line, which allows the angler to "swim the minnow" in a natural fashion.

Full sinking lines do have their place in the angler's repertoire. Slow sinking lines are very effective in still water situations. Beach cutthroating , lake and slough fishing all will, at some point, require the use of full sinking lines. In rivers, most line control is lost when the line sinks. When an upstream cast is made with the fast full sinking line, the angler really doesn't have any idea how the fly is "fishing" because of the effects of currents and eddies.

Sinking tip fly lines round out the angler's collection of lines. Available in short four-foot sinking tip sections or the longer thirty-foot sink tip. For cutthroat fishing, the short sink tip, from four to sixteen feet, is ample. These lines come in various sink rates and, ideally, the faster the sink rate the better. The fly line leader should be kept very short, less than five feet, in moving water situations. The combination of the fast sinking tip and short leader, with proper line manipulation, will keep the fly near the bottom and the feeding fish.

Spring Sea-runs

Spring cutthroat fishing brings warmer water temperatures and more actively feeding fish. On some large river systems, such as the Harrison, fish and fishermen eagerly await the emergence of salmon fry. During mild winters and warmer early springs, the salmon fry emergence can be much earlier. Water temperatures just one or two degrees above normal can speed up the hatching time. First to emerge are the pink salmon fry, progeny from the previous year's adults. On the south coast, in odd-numbered years, adult pink salmon make their way into many of our coastal rivers. In the spring following, the young of these salmon migrate directly to the sea. Waiting to intercept are the hungry cutthroat. Some of the larger mature cutts are on the mend after undergoing the rigors of spawning. Feeding voraciously, these sea-runs attack the schools of salmon fry, head pointed upstream drifting with the current, on their journey to the sea.

For the fly angler this is a very exciting time to fish. Fishing is more visual as the cutthroat slash through the schools of moving fry. The cutts are easy to locate as they force the fry to the surface, like hungry salmon chasing herring. A small minnow imitation works well for this situation. Most fish are just under the surface, and a steady foot-long retrieve in still water should bring results. Free-swimming fry congregate in large schools, always facing upstream, unable to swim against the current. Look for eddies and riffles—areas that will trap the fry and serve them to the waiting trout. When cutts are on salmon fry they will show, often with very splashy rises.

Once while fishing the Harrison River, I came across a school of feeding cutthroat. Standing on one of the river's many bars, I watched as the wind blew upriver making large waves. Inside the waves, back lit by the setting sun, were the silver trout, surfing and eating fry. As spring advances and the chum salmon fry emerge, the rivers are full of downstream out-migrants. The cutthroat can be very selective at this time and the fly angler should fish early and late in the day, taking advantage of low light conditions.

Sea-run cutthroat can be found in all the rivers and streams that have salmon runs. Rivers with the largest, most diverse runs, have the biggest concentrations of cutthroat. The Stave River has a huge run of chums and good populations of cutthroat in the spring. The Vedder Canal, which passes under the Trans-Canada Highway near Chilliwack, B.C., has excellent trout fishing when the salmon fry are migrating. The Harrison River system is made up of a series of head water, glacier-fed streams feeding into Lillooet Lake, Lillooet River and, finally, forty-mile-long Harrison Lake. The lake itself, along its eastern and western shores, has some great cutthroat fishing in April. Below the lake, at its outlet, the Harrison gradually picks up speed, then slows above the confluence of Morris Slough. Below the slough, the first long fingers of gravel jut out from shore. This is where the odd-year pinks spawn and the early spring cutthroat wait, eating stone flies until the pink fry emerge. Anchoring the boat and casting a tied-down minnow fly toward shore will often produce fish. At Cabin Point you can climb the rock and gaze into the crystal clear water. Watch the fry as they come swirling around the corner out of control, held by the current. Up from the pebble bottom, ten feet down, come the cutthroat rising and scattering the panicked fry. I have come to this spot many times just to watch the fish feed before casting my fly in the frantic instant when the cutts are slashing through the fry. When the sea-runs have been feeding on fry for a while, they can become very selective, especially in slow-moving water. Size and color of the fly are important, particularly size.

Further downriver, below the highway bridge, the Harrison broadens into a large bay. The bay is a catchment for juvenile salmon and stickle backs. During high water, the river eddies around the bay almost imperceptibly, and the salmon fry group up in large schools. Sea-runs come to the bay for this springtime feast. Cruising the muddy flats, these hunters search out the fry, rushing their prey in a visual display of surface activity. The best fly line for this situation is the slow-sinking or intermediate line. A specific line, made by Scientific Anglers called the Stillwater, is particularly good for this type of fishing. The line is transparent, which is excellent for casting to spooky fish. Some fly patterns the angler should have include the Tied Down Minnow, Egg 'n' I and small Silver Streamers. (Always cast to any surface disturbance that you see. After the cast is made, before you let the line sink,

137

strip in a few feet of fly line. This will allow you to detect a strike as the fly is sinking.)

The river surges and boils now, as it hits the mountain and travels under the train bridge in the home stretch on the way to its meeting with the Fraser. At the confluence, a gray line is drawn as the Fraser pushes to mix with the clear green Harrison. It is spring and although the Fraser is not yet in full blown freshet, both rivers are carrying millions of young salmon on their journey to the sea.

Summer Beach Trout

As spring progresses to summer and the smaller streams shrivel and lose most of their water, the cutthroat head for the sea and all the food it has to offer. As the sea-runs move into the estuaries, they branch out moving along the shore lines in search of food. Some areas, such as Crescent Beach in the Lower Mainland, have great fishing in the month of June. Try down toward the southwest point on the ebb tide. This tide is best, because during the flood tide eel grass and other debris tend to foul the hook. For the angler with a boat, access to many beaches is achieved. I prefer not to fish out of the boat, but often use it to cover a lot of area quickly. Resident populations of sea-run cutthroat can still be found in the densely populated areas of the Lower Mainland. Unfortunately, we have lost many of the tiny individual streams that cutthroat depend upon.

East of the Second Narrows Bridge, on the north and south side, good beaches abound. Some are near industrial areas and for access are best fished at low tide. The more pristine areas are found further up the inlet, where steep mountain slopes fall directly to the sea. Between the mountains tiny rivulets carve out the rock and come together to form the stream. In the estuary, thousands of years of erosion have deposited the small gravel to form the cutthroat beach. Eel grass grows here in small patches where the cobble turns to sand. Among the swaying grasses, tiny sculpins dart around and then seek cover as the cutthroat arrive.

I had checked three beaches since leaving Rocky Point boat launch without seeing a single fish. This beach was my fourth and last for the evening. Weaving between the crab traps, I idled the boat to within a few feet of shore. The tide was rising, flooding the little tidal pools with water, the tiny grains of dry sand floating on top. I quietly lowered the anchor, making sure that there was enough slack in the anchor line so that the boat would not drift away with the rising tide. Sliding into the warm water, wearing just shorts and running shoes, I made my way to shore. At the north end of the beach, a shallow channel surrounded a small island. The light was going fast, with the August sun already down behind the mountains. The channel around the island was filled now, and I knew if the cutts were here, this is the way they would come. A warm gentle breeze rippled the water. I tied on a small deer hair dry fly and cast it into the channel. With the breeze at my back, the little fly turned over and the twelve-foot leader laid out straight. Suddenly, without warning, in a long arcing curve, he pounced on it—taking the fly on his way down into the water. On the reel instantly, the sea-run was into the fly line backing, tearing along the surface pushing a bow wave of water. After a series of leaps, the hook fell out and I could only think that this fish was not one of the usual resident cutthroat. Seven sea-runs came to the fly that August evening, all the same size and all of them beautiful. Golden yellow and covered with sea lice, I wondered where these fish had come from. Had they followed the pinks that were just making their way into the Indian River? For two weeks the cutthroat were at that beach and then, like nomads, they were gone.

August, September and October are the prime months for beach cutthroating. On the Sunshine Coast, fish can be found at or near any of the dozens of creeks that flow into Howe Sound or Georgia Strait. Some of the beaches are popular swimming areas and are best fished early when the sun comes up. Porpoise Bay Provincial Park has good camping and an excellent beach. A popular area, it is best to wait until after Labor Day to fish. Using a small car-top boat the angler can reach many beaches that are only accessible by boat. Spend some time exploring, as it is the only prerequisite to finding that hidden cutthroat beach.

Urban Cutthroat

The burgeoning population of the Lower Mainland has not been easy on the cutthroat trout. Urban sprawl has enveloped the southwest coast and is rapidly spreading eastward. Tiny creeks are covered over by asphalt—streams that were the only home to distinct populations of cutthroat. Some larger streams have survived relatively unscathed, due to the persistence of concerned individuals and the Ministry of the Environment's dedicated employees who struggle with meager funding to satisfy the needs of all interested parties. The needs of the cutthroat are simple: clear, clean water and unobstructed waterways to the sea. Greenbelts and parklike settings are all part of the 1990s urban developments. Small streams need to be protected. Stream-side vegetation must be left intact to cool the summer flows and provide cover. As more people become environmentally aware, there has been and will be positive change in the treatment of our rivers and streams. People have more time for outdoor activities and even if one of their pursuits isn't fly fishing for cutthroat, everyone wants clean water in natural surroundings.

A sea-run cutthroat symposium was held in Reedsport, Oregon, in 1995. Some of the findings of that meeting were grim. Through urbanization and the resulting loss of habitats, some stocks have become extinct. These stocks of sea-run cutthroat have disappeared within the last ten years. Cutthroat trout stocks on the south coast of B.C. have been the hardest hit. Lower Mainland and southeastern Vancouver Island streams have lost fifteen different stocks of sea-runs. Numerous other streams may suffer the same fate if people aren't made more aware of the importance of even the smallest urban stream. On a more positive note, cutthroat, being the nomadic trout that they are, can repopulate a stream that is barren.

Some populations of cutthroat are in trouble because of over fishing. Fortunately, the biologists and technicians working for the B. C. Ministry of Environment could see the writing on the wall, and anticipating the increased angling pressure, implemented a no-kill regulation on all wild sea-run cutthroat trout. Through hatchery stockings, pressure was taken off the dwindling wild stocks of cutthroat—a bold move, and a win-win situation for the wild cutthroat and people wanting to take fish home. The Department of Fisheries and Oceans has also protected the sea-run in its saltwater environment. Today, no wild trout or char south of a line due west from Cape Caution may be kept. All wild trout must be released and only those trout of hatchery origin can be retained. Hatchery marked fish are distinguished by the missing adipose fin (a small fleshy fin in front of the tail). Trout that are kept must be larger than eleven and three-quarters inches and the daily limit is two. If the angler wishes to keep fish, he or she should consider releasing larger trout of sixteen to twenty inches in length. Females of this size will carry thousands of eggs that produce the sea-run cutthroat for the future generations of fish and fishermen.

Cutthroat stocks on the mid to north coast and Queen Charlotte Islands are thriving due to their remoteness, although some streams are suffering from some habitat degradation. In the northern part of the province, very few studies have been done on the sea-run cutthroat. Literally hundreds of cutthroat streams flow to the sea making it a monumental task to catalogue all of them.

Hooked on Sea-runs

When I was a young teenager, my father would take me on frequent trips to the Sunshine Coast. We would stop in Gibsons so that he could visit with friends. Being the ever-fanatical fisherman, I was always looking for places to fish. I had just recently taken up fly fishing and was eager to try my new fly outfit. After a seemingly endless conversation, my father's friend decided to take us down to his place of employment. I knew that he worked as a dozer boat operator on the booming grounds northeast of the Langdale ferry terminal. I wasn't overly thrilled to be around a bunch of log booms, but at least there was water and maybe a place to fish.

Within a few minutes we were snaking our way down the gravel road that led to the log sort at tide water. Twin creeks, one on each side of the winding road, raced beside us. At the bridge, the two creeks intertwined and, as one, emptied into the bay. We parked the car just inside the gate, my father and his friend making their way into the office. I threw on my old rubber waders, grabbed my rod and ran back to the bridge.

The water in the creek under the bridge was the color of tea. I dangled my fly off the bridge down into the little pool formed by the bridge footings. I watched as the orange fly drifted in the current, it reached the tail out and bounced on top of the waves. "Looks like an orange stick," I thought, as I reeled in my line. I jumped down from the bridge cribbing and instead of bush whacking my way through the brambles, I decided to walk the creek the last 200 yards to the beach. At tide water, I was relieved to feel the traction that the barnacle encrusted rocks gave me after slipping and sliding my way down the creek bed. The estuary was not particularly beautiful; the tide was out and chunks of tree bark lay everywhere on the muddy flat. I made my way to the water's edge trying not to sink in the sticky mud. The ground was firmer when I was in the water, and there was only about sixty feet casting distance to the log booms. Off to one side in the water in front of me was an old boom log, its rusty anchor chain hanging off both ends. At first, I flailed the water in front of me trying to make a decent forty-foot cast. Then I remembered I had read somewhere that sea-run cutthroat prefer the cover that floating logs provide. I immediately picked up the floating fly line and, after numerous false casts, proceeded to place the fly on the end of the log! A few curse words later, I gently flicked the line and to my surprise it came off the log. The "orange stick fly" was running parallel to the log as I retrieved it. I was not ready when that big yellow trout came out from under that old log. He grabbed the fly and greyhounded off, breaking my wind knotted leader and leaving me shaking. At thirteen, this was my introduction to beach sea-run cutthroat fishing.

This beach, like many others, has changed over the years. The creek was diverted and now has its estuary further away from the booming grounds—a change for the better.

The sea-run cutthroat trout is a wonderful fish. The pursuit of this challenging trout will test the skill of every fly angler through spring, summer, fall and winter. Truly a trout for all seasons, angling for cutthroat will take you for a quiet stroll on a pebble beach or a walk in a moss-covered rainforest. Natural surroundings enhance the fishing experience...the fish are the bonus.

British Columbia
Coastal Cutthroat Trout Distribution

Numbers correspond to Fisheries Management Regions.

Playing a cutthroat in Clayquot Sound on Vancouver Island. A virtual oasis of never-ending gently sloping gravel beaches.   *Photo: Harry Penner*

Above: Kelly Davison searching for the elusive sea-run, looking for any movement that may indicate the cutthroat are there!

Right: Kelly Davison casting to the elusive sea-run in its saltwater environment.

Below: Kelly Davison brings a brightly colored sea-run cutthroat trout to the beach.

Photos: Harry Penner

Above: Kelly Davison holds a brightly speckled anadromous cutthroat trout.

Right: This sea-run took to a skated dry fly on an early June morning.

Below: A vividly colored sea-run cutthroat in hand.

Photos: Harry Penner

147

Left: In the search for the elusive sea-run the fish are the bonus. Kelly Davison still wears a smile after twenty years of pursuing his sea-run passion.

Below: Fly fishing the backwaters of the Fraser River in the Fraser Valley during the winter months.

Photos: Harry Penner

Gently sloping beaches, with small gravel—a perfect environment for the sea-run cutthroat.

Photo: Harry Penner

Above: Sea-run cutthroat with a disclike parasite that is common with these anadromous fish.　　*Photo: Harry Penner*

Following page: Estuaries of rivers at a low tide flooding in can provide spectacular results as the sea-runs wait for the thousands of salmon fry to leave their home rivers in the spring each year.

Photo: Harry Penner

More Great Hancock House Titles

Steelhead
Barry Thornton
ISBN 0-88839-370-9
5½ x 8½, 192 pp.

Saltwater Flyfishing for Pacific Salmon
Barry Thornton
ISBN 0-88839-268-0
5½ x 8½, 168 pp.

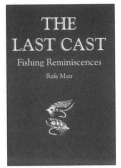

The Last Cast: Fishing Reminiscences
Rafe Mair
ISBN 0-88839-346-6
5½ x 8½, 160 pp.

Mooching: The Salmon Fisherman's Bible
David Nuttall
ISBN 0-88839-097-1
5½ x 8½, 184 pp.

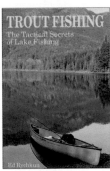

Trout Fishing
Ed Rychkun
ISBN 0-88839-338-5
5½ x 8½, 120 pp.

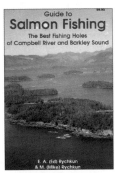

Guide to Salmon Fishing
Ed Rychkun
ISBN 0-88839-305-9
5½ x 8½, 96 pp.

West Coast River Angling
Eric Carlisle
ISBN 0-88839-212-5
5½ x 8½, 192 pp.

195 Lakes of the Fraser Valley Vol. I
Ed Rychkun
ISBN 0-88839-339-3
5½ x 8½, 238 pp.

195 Lakes of the Fraser Valley Vol. II
Ed Rychkun
ISBN 0-88839-377-6
5½ x 8½, 272 pp.